Table of Contents

Using this Guide

This book is a *guide* for teachers using the *Primary Mathematics* curriculum. It is designed to help teachers understand the course material, to see how each section fits in with the curriculum as a whole, and to prepare the day's lesson. The course material is divided into 72 sessions. Sessions can be combined for one day's lesson by spending less time on class participation or discussion or not having as many problems for practice during class time.

This guide is designed to be used with both the U.S. edition and the third edition of *Primary Mathematics*. U.S. conventions and spellings are used in this guide, such as using commas for thousands and colons for time, and not using "and" in writing out whole numbers in words. However, any items specific to either edition, such as different answers, different page numbers, and different exercise numbers, are indicated with a superscript **US** or **3d**.

Workbook exercises can be gone over in class or assigned as homework.

This guide schedules reviews as blocks of several successive sessions. However, you can have a review session every few weeks instead, using selected problems from the textbook and workbook review exercises.

Suggested Material

Number discs

These are discs with 0.001, 0.01, 0.1, 1, 10, 100, 1000, 10,000, and 100,000 written on them. Have some that can be displayed; you can write the numbers on transparent counters if you have an overhead projector. You can also simply draw circles on the board and label them. For student manipulatives, you can write the numbers on opaque counters. Each student or group should have 18 of each type.

10 x 10 grids

For students, copy the ones from this guide, or use the backs of laminated hundreds boards. For displayable 10 x 10 grids copy the ones from this guide onto transparent sheets that can be used with an overhead projector, or you can use overhead blank hundreds boards. Sets of overhead fraction squares include squares divided into ten columns and rows, so you could use that instead.

Counters

Use the opaque round counters that will fit on a hundreds board, or cubes, or any suitable counter. They should be in 4-5 different colors.

Measuring tools

Meter sticks, yard sticks, rulers, protractors, set squares (plastic triangles with 90°-45°-45° or 90°-30°-60° angles), stopwatch, postage scale (optional), graduated cylinder, liter measuring cup, 100 ml graduated cylinder or beaker.

Base-10 blocks

A set with unit cubes, rods (10 units), flats (10 rods), and a cube (10 flats). Use ones that can be displayed from the front of the class (such as using an overhead projector or ones that can be stuck onto the board). You can also just draw them on the board.

Multilink cubes

Cubes such as Connect-A-Cubes® which connect on all 6 sides to form 2-dimensional figures.

Optional Resources

Wiggle Woods CD-ROM

This CD-ROM contains learning activities and two games. The name of the program refers to the bug theme. Topics covered include material from both Primary Mathematics 5 and 6. The following chart correlates the different activities to the appropriate part of *Primary Mathematics 5B*.

Primary Mathematics 5B		***Wiggle Woods Primary Five***
Unit 1 – Decimals	Part 3 – Division by Tens, Hundreds or Thousands	Game 1: Levels 2-3
	Part 5 – Conversion of Measurements	Game 1: Level 4
Unit 2 – Percentage	Part 1 – Percent	Percentage: Learn and Explore
	Part 2 – Writing Fractions as Percentages	Percentage: Activity
	Part 3 – Percentage of a Quantity	Percentage: Challenge Game 1: Level 5
Unit 6 – Triangles	Part 2 – Isosceles and Equilateral Triangles	Game 2: Matchstick puzzles
Unit 8 – Tessellations	Part 1 – Tiling Patterns	Game 3: Tessellations

Supplemental Workbooks

These optional workbooks provide a source of extra problems for more practice, tests, and class discussions. Some have interesting and thought-provoking non-routine problems for discussion.

Extra Practice for Primary Mathematics 5 (U.S. Edition)
This workbook has two to four page exercises covering topics from *Primary Mathematics 5A* and *Primary Mathematics 5B*. The level of difficulty and format of the problems is similar to that of the *Primary Mathematics*. Answers are in the back.

Primary Mathematics Challenging Word Problems 5 (U.S. Edition)
This workbook has word problems only. The problems are topically arranged, with the topics following the same sequence as *Primary Mathematics 5A* and *5B*. Each topic starts with three worked examples, followed by practice problems and then challenge problems. Although the computation skills needed to solve the problems is at the same level as the corresponding *Primary Mathematics*, the problem solving techniques necessary in the challenge section are sometimes more advanced, with the problems requiring more steps to solve. It is a good source, of extra word problems that can be discussed in class or of enrichment problems for more capable students. Answers are in the back.

Primary Mathematics Intensive Practice 5B (U.S. Edition)
This supplemental workbook has one set of problems for each topic in *Primary Mathematics*. Each topical exercise has questions of varying levels of difficulty, but the difficulty level is usually higher than that in the *Primary Mathematics* textbook or workbook. Some of the word problems are quite challenging and require the students to extend their understanding of the concepts and develop problem solving abilities. There is also a section called "Take the Challenge!" with non-routine problems that can be used to further develop students' problem solving abilities. Answers are located in the back.

This page is blank.

Unit 1 – Decimals

Objectives

- Round a decimal number to 2 decimal places.
- Divide a decimal number by a 1-digit whole number.
- Express a fraction as a decimal number correct to 2 decimal places.
- Multiply and divide decimal numbers by tens, hundreds, and thousands.
- Multiply a decimal number of up to 2 places by a 2-digit whole number.
- Convert measurements involving decimal numbers.

Suggested number of sessions: 16

	Objectives	Textbook	Workbook	Activities
Part 1 : Approximation and Estimation				**4 sessions**
1	▪ Review decimal numbers and fractions.	p. 22, Review A, 1-4, 7, 9-10		1.1a
2	▪ Round decimal numbers to 2 decimal places. ▪ Review dividing a decimal number by a whole number.	p. 6 pp. 6-7, tasks 1-2 p. 22, Review A, 5	Ex. 1	1.1b
3	▪ Divide a decimal number by a 1-digit whole number and round the quotient to 2 decimal places.	p. 7, tasks 3-4	Ex. 2	1.1c
4	▪ Express a fraction as a decimal number correct to 2 decimal places.	p. 7, tasks 5-6 p. 22, Review A, 6	Ex. 3	1.1d
Part 2 : Multiplication by Tens, Hundreds or Thousands				**3 sessions**
5	▪ Multiply a decimal number by 10. ▪ Multiply a decimal number by tens.	p. 8 p. 9, tasks 1-4 p. 10, tasks 5-6	Ex. 4	1.2a
6	▪ Multiply a decimal number by 100. ▪ Multiply a decimal number by 1000.	p. 10, tasks 7-8 p. 11, tasks 9-11	Ex. 5	1.2b
7	▪ Multiply a decimal number by hundreds or thousands.	p. 11, tasks 12-14 p. 22, Review A, 8(a)-8(c)	Ex. 6	1.2c
Part 3 : Division by Tens, Hundreds or Thousands				**3 sessions**
8	▪ Divide a decimal number by 10. ▪ Divide a decimal number by tens.	p. 12 p. 13, tasks 1-4 p. 14, tasks 5-6	Ex. 7	1.3a
9	▪ Divide a decimal number by 100. ▪ Divide a decimal number by 1000.	p. 14, tasks 7-8 p. 15, tasks 9-11	Ex. 8	1.3b
10	▪ Divide a decimal number by hundreds or thousands.	p. 15, tasks 12-14 p. 22, Review A, 8(d)-8(f)	Ex. 9	1.3c

	Objectives	Textbook	Workbook	Activities
Part 4 : Multiplying by a 2-digit Whole Number				**2 sessions**
11	▪ Estimate the product in multiplication of decimal numbers. ▪ Multiply a decimal number of up to 2 decimal places by a 2-digit whole number.	p. 16 p. 17, task 1	Ex. 10	1.4a
12	▪ Multiply a decimal number of up to 2 decimal places by a 2-digit whole number.	p. 17, tasks 2-3	Ex. 11	1.4b
Part 5 : Conversion of Measurements				**4 sessions**
13	▪ Convert a measurement in a decimal number to a smaller unit. ▪ Convert a measurement in a decimal number to a compound unit.	p. 18 p. 19, tasks 1-5	Ex. 12	1.5a
14	▪ Convert a measurement smaller than the conversion factor to a larger unit.	p. 20, tasks 6-10	Ex. 13	1.5b
15	▪ Convert a measurement greater than the conversion factor to a larger unit.	p. 20, tasks 11-12 p. 22, Review A, 11	Ex. 14	1.5c
16	▪ Practice.	p. 21, Practice 1A		1.5d

Part 1: Approximation and Estimation — 4 sessions

Objectives

- Review decimal numbers.
- Round decimal numbers to 2 decimal places.
- Divide a decimal number by a 1-digit whole number and round the quotient to 2 decimal places.
- Express a fraction as a decimal number correct to 2 decimal places.

Materials

- Number discs (discs with 0.001, 0.01, 0.1, 1, 10, and 100 written on them)

Homework

- Workbook Exercise 1
- Workbook Exercise 2
- Workbook Exercise 3

Notes

In *Primary Mathematics 4B*, students learned to round decimal numbers to one decimal place. This is extended here to rounding decimal numbers to 2 decimal places. The process is similar for rounding to 3 or more decimal places.

To round a number to a certain place value, look first at the digit in the next lower place. If that lower-place-value digit is 5 or more, increase the digit in the place being rounded to by 1. If that lower-place-value digit is 4 or less, do not change the digit in the place value that the number is being rounded to. All digits to the right of this to the digit in the place being rounded to are changed to 0. Any of these 0's that are past the decimal point can be dropped. For example:

345.631 is 300 when rounded to the nearest hundred.
345.631 is 350 when rounded to the nearest ten.
345.631 is 346 when rounded to the nearest whole number.
345.631 is 345.6 when rounded to the nearest tenth.
345.631 is 345.63 when rounded to the nearest hundredth.

Students should have a good understanding of decimal numbers to thousandths.

In *Primary Mathematics 4B*, the division algorithm, which was learned in *Primary Mathematics 3A*, was extended to division of a decimal number by a 1-digit whole number. Students learned to round the quotient to 1-decimal place by first dividing to 2 decimal places, and then rounding to 1 decimal place. Here, students will divide out to 3 decimal places, in order to be able to round correctly to 2 decimal places.

In *Primary Mathematics 5A*, students learned to relate fractions to division. They also learned to convert an improper fraction (a fraction with a numerator equal to or larger than the denominator) into a mixed number or whole number, using division to do so. Here, instead of writing the remainder as a fraction, they will divide the fractional part and express the quotient as a decimal number correct to 2 decimal places.

Activity 1.1a **Review**

1. Review place-value and decimal numbers.
   - Remind students that the value of a digit in a number depends on its place in relation to the decimal point. Each digit in a number has a value that is ten times the value of the same digit one place to its right, and a value that is $\frac{1}{10}$ the value of the same digit one place to its left.

   ÷10 ÷10 ÷10 ÷10 ÷10 ÷10

   1 1 1 1 . 1 1 1

   x10 x10 x10 x10 x10 x10

   - Write the number 123.456. Ask students for the value of the digit 3, which is in the first place to the left (just before) the decimal point. It is 3 ones. Ask them for the value of the digit 2, which is one place further to the left. It is 2×10, 20, or 2 tens. Note that when we write 20, we need the 0 to show we have 2 tens, not 2 ones. Similarly, the value of the digit 1 is $1 \times 10 \times 10$, or 1×100, or 1 hundred.
   - Ask students for the value of the digit 4, which is in the first decimal place. It is 1 x $\frac{1}{10}$, or $\frac{1}{10}$ of 4, or 4 tenths. Similarly, the value of the digit 5 is $\frac{1}{100}$ of 5, or 5 hundredths. The value of the digit 6 is $\frac{1}{1000}$ of 6, or 6 thousandths.
   - Show students how the number can be written in expanded form, or, more simply, as the sum of the values of each digit.

   $$123.456 = (1 \times 100) + (2 \times 10) + (3 \times 1) + (4 \times \frac{1}{10}) + (5 \times \frac{1}{100}) + (6 \times \frac{1}{1000})$$
   $$123.456 = 100 + 20 + 3 + \frac{4}{10} + \frac{5}{100} + \frac{6}{1000}$$

   - Provide another example, such as 600.304, where some of the digits are 0.
   - Point out that when we write the expanded form, we do not customarily write a fraction for a 0, but they don have to realize that a fraction of 100 is missing, so 0 will be in the hundredths place. We could write the fraction $\frac{0}{100}$ to remind ourselves that there is a 0 in that place.

   $$600.304 = 600 + \frac{3}{10} + \frac{4}{1000}$$
   $$600.304 = 600 + \frac{3}{10} + \frac{0}{100} + \frac{4}{1000}$$

2. Have students do **problems 1-4, 7** and **9-10**, **Review A, textbook p. 22**. Review order of operations if necessary.

Activity 1.1b **Round to 2 decimal places**

1. Discuss rounding to hundredths.
   - Discuss the contents of **textbook p. 6,** including **task 1**.
   - Point out the wavy equal sign ≈, which can be read as "is about."
   - Have students do **tasks 2, textbook p. 7**

2. Review rounding to other places.
   - Have students round the numbers in task 2 to tenths, ones, and tens.
   - Provide some numbers, such as 951.6, that have digits in the hundreds place and have students round them to various places.

3. Review division.
   - Step through a division problem, such as 951.6 ÷ 5, where the quotient will have more place values than the divided (the number being divided).
     - Divide 9 hundreds by 5. The quotient is 1 hundred and the remainder is 4 hundreds.
     - Rename the 4 hundreds as 40 tens and add to it the 5 tens ("bring down" the 5). Divide 45 tens by 5. The quotient is 9 tens and the remainder is 0 tens
     - Since the remainder is 0, there is only 1 one to divide. It cannot be divided by 5, so the quotient for ones is 0, and the remainder is 1.
     - Rename the 1 one as 10 tenths and add to it the 6 tenths ("bring down" the 6). Divide 16 tenths by 5. The quotient is 3 tenths and the remainder is 1 tenth.
     - Rename the tenth as 10 hundredths. Divide 10 hundredths by 5. The quotient is 2 hundredths and there is no remainder.
   - Have students to **problem 5, Review A, p. 22** or a few other division problems you supply where the quotient terminates within 3 decimal places.

```
   1
5)9 5 1. 6
 -5
  4
   ↓
  1 9
5)9 5 1. 6
  5
  4 5
 -4 5
    0
    ↓
  1 9 0.
5)9 5 1. 6
  5
  4 5
 -4 5
    0 1
      ↓
  1 9 0. 3
5)9 5 1. 6
  5
  4 5
 -4 5
    0 1  6
  -   1  5
         1
      ↓
  1 9 0. 3 2
5)9 5 1. 6 0
  5
  4 5
 -4 5
    0 1  6
  -   1  5
         1 0
        -1 0
           0
```

Workbook Exercise 1

Activity 1.1c **Round the quotient to 2 decimal places**

1. Discuss rounding the quotient of a division problem.
   - Step through a problem such as 22 ÷ 7 where the quotient is a non-terminating decimal. Carry out the division to at least hundredths.
   - Tell students that in problems that involve decimals, we often use an approximate answer, either when the answer does not have to be so precise past a certain place value, or where it is not possible to get an exact answer, as when the decimal does not terminate.
   - Ask students to round the quotient for 22 ÷ 7 to a whole number. To round to a whole number, we use the digit in the tenths place. Lead them to see that if we are asked to find an answer to a division problem, correct to a whole number, we need to find the quotient to the tenth to know whether to round up or down.
   - Ask students to round the quotient to a tenth. Point out that to do so, we use the digit in the hundredth place. So, if are asked to find an answer to a division problem correct to 1 decimal place, we need to find the quotient to 2 decimal places in order to be able to round to 1 decimal place.
   - Ask students to round the quotient to a hundredth. We need to use the value in the thousandth place. So, to find a quotient correct 2 decimal places, we need to find the quotient to 3 decimal places.
   - Discuss **task 3, textbook p. 7**.

```
    3.142 ...
7)22.0
  21
   10
    7
    30
    28
     20
     14
      6
```

Workbook Exercise 2

Activity 1.1d **Round the quotient to 2 decimal places**

1. Review fraction and division.
   - Remind students that a fraction is another way of writing a division problem.
   - We can use division to convert an improper fraction to a mixed number. For example, in 9 ÷ 4, there is a remainder of 1. If that remainder is further divided into 4 equal groups, each group would get $\frac{1}{4}$. Instead of writing the answer to the division problem as 2 with a remainder of 1, we can write it as $2\frac{1}{4}$.
   - We can also carry the division out farther and get a decimal quotient.
   - If we start with the mixed number, $2\frac{1}{4}$, we can convert this to a decimal by performing the division 1 ÷ 4.

$3 \div 4 = \frac{3}{4}$

```
  2
4)9
  8
  1
```

$\frac{9}{4} = 9 \div 4 = 2\frac{1}{4}$

```
  2.25
4)9.00
  8
  10
   8
   20
   20
    0
```

2. Discuss **task 5, textbook p. 7**.

3. Have students do **task 6, textbook p. 7**.
   - You can have students do **problem 6, Review A, textbook p. 22** for more practice.

4. Students should eventually become familiar with the decimal representation of some common fractions. List some common fractions and have students convert them to decimals.

$\frac{1}{2} = 0.5$

$\frac{1}{3} = 0.333...$ $\quad \frac{2}{3} = 0.666...$

$\frac{1}{4} = 0.25$ $\quad \frac{3}{4} = 3 \times \frac{1}{4} = 0.75$

$\frac{1}{5} = 0.2$ $\quad \frac{2}{5} = 2 \times 0.2 = 0.4$ $\quad \frac{3}{5} = 3 \times 0.2 = 0.6$ $\quad \frac{4}{5} = 4 \times 0.2 = 0.8$

$\frac{1}{6} = 0.1666...$ $\quad \frac{1}{8} = 0.125$

5. Discuss simplifying fractions or division problems before dividing.
   - Write the problem 210 ÷ 56 and ask for suggestions on how to make this problem simpler.
   - Show how we can first write it as a fraction, simplify, and then divide. We can simplify in steps; for example, we can recognize that both 210 and 56 are multiples of 7 and start by dividing the numerator and denominator by 7 to get the simpler fraction $\frac{30}{8}$, which can be further simplified to $\frac{15}{4}$.

$$210 \div 56 = \frac{210}{56} = \frac{30}{8} = \frac{15}{4} = 3\frac{3}{4} = 3.75$$

Workbook Exercise 3

Part 2: Multiplication by Tens, Hundreds or Thousands **3 sessions**

Objectives

- Multiply a decimal number by tens, hundreds, or thousands

Materials

- Number discs (discs with 0.001, 0.01, 0.1, 1, 10, and 100 written on them)

Homework

- Workbook Exercise 4
- Workbook Exercise 5
- Workbook Exercise 6

Notes

In *Primary Mathematics 4A*, students learned to multiply a whole number by tens, hundreds, and thousands. Here, the concepts are extended to decimals.

When a whole number is multiplied by 10, a 0 is added to the whole number. Each digit is moved to the next higher place value, and a 0 is added in the one's place.

$1{,}234 \times 10 = 12{,}34\mathbf{0}$

When a decimal is multiplied by 10, the digits are also moved to the next higher place value. As a result, the decimal point has moved one place to the right and each digit is now ten times as much as it was.

$1.234 \times 10 = 1\mathbf{2}.34$

When a whole number is multiplied by 100, the digits are moved two places to the left, and two 0's are added to the whole number. That is, the decimal point has moved two places to the right.

$1{,}234 \times 100 = 123{,}4\mathbf{00}$

When a decimal is multiplied by 100, again the digits are moved two places to the left, adding a 0 if necessary. The value of each digit is now a hundred times as much.

$1.234 \times 100 = 1\mathbf{23}.4$

$1.2 \times 100 = 1\mathbf{20}$

When a whole number or decimal number is multiplied by 1000, each digit is moved three places to the left, adding 0's if necessary. The value of each digit is now 1000 times as much as it was previously. As a result, the decimal point has been moved three places to the right.

$1{,}234 \times 1000 = 1{,}234{,}\mathbf{000}$

$1.234 \times 1000 = 1\mathbf{234}$

$1.2 \times 1000 = 1\mathbf{200}$

$1.23 \times 1000 = 1\mathbf{230}$

To multiply a number by tens, hundreds, or thousands, we can do it in steps; first multiplying by the non-zero digit in the tens place, and then multiplying by 10, 100, or 1000.

$$\begin{aligned} 4.3 \times 200 &= 4.3 \times 2 \times 100 \\ &= 8.6 \times 100 \\ &= 860 \end{aligned}$$

Activity 1.2a **Multiply by tens**

1. Illustrate multiplying a decimal number by 10.
   - Refer to **textbook p. 8**. Use number discs to illustrate the process.
   - Guide students to see that each tenth, when multiplied by 10, becomes a one.

     1 tenth x 10 = 1 one
     8 tenths x 10 = 8 ones
     0.8 x 10 = 8
   - Each hundredth, when multiplied by 10, becomes a tenth.

     1 hundredth x 10 = 1 tenth
     8 hundredths x 10 = 8 tenths
     0.08 x 10 = 0.8
   - Each thousandth, when multiplied by 10, becomes a hundredth.

     1 thousandth x 10 = 1 hundredth
     8 thousandths x 10 = 8 hundredths
     0.008 x 10 = 0.08
   - Have students illustrate **task 1, textbook p. 9** with number discs and find the products.
   - Discuss **task 2, textbook p. 9**. Each digit is multiplied by 10.
   - Discuss **task 3, textbook p. 9**. Illustrate with number discs.
     - Students should see that when a decimal number is multiplied by 10, we move the decimal point one place to the right. This causes the digit in each place to be multiplied by ten; that is, each digit moves to one place to the left, where its value is now ten times its original value.

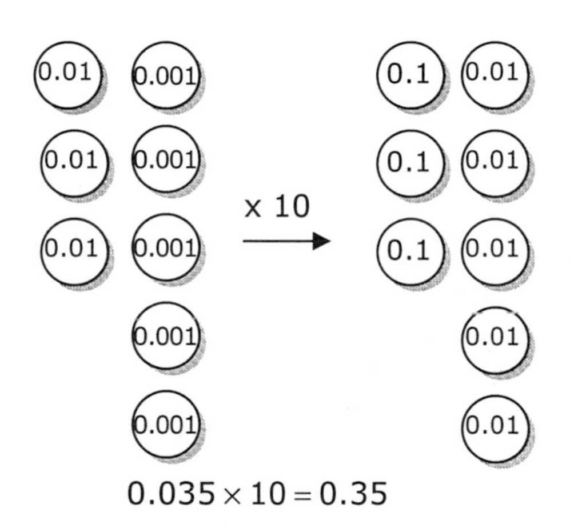

$0.035 \times 10 = 0.35$

2. Have students do **task 4, textbook p. 9**.

3. Discuss multiplying by tens.
   - Write a multiplication problem involving multiplication of a decimal number by ones. Have students solve the problem mentally or with the multiplication algorithm.

     $0.45 \times 3 = 1.35$
   - Write the same problem, except multiply by tens instead. Show students how to do the problem in two steps. Point out that to multiply by 30, we can multiply by 3, and then move the decimal point over one place.

     0.45×30

     $0.45 \xrightarrow{\times 3} 1.35 \xrightarrow{\times 10} 13.5$
   - We can also first multiply by 10 and then by the digit in the tens place. This can sometimes make the mental computation easier.

     $$\begin{aligned} 0.45 \times 30 &= 0.45 \times 10 \times 3 \\ &= 4.5 \times 3 \\ &= 13.5 \end{aligned}$$

4. Have students do **tasks 5-6, textbook p. 10**.

Workbook Exercise 4

Activity 1.2b **Multiply by 100 and 1000**

1. Illustrate multiplying a decimal number by 100 and 1000.
   - Refer to **task 7, textbook p. 10**. Illustrate with number discs.
   - Lead students to see that each thousandth, when multiplied by 100, becomes a tenth. You can show that multiplying a thousandth by 10 gives a hundredth (10 thousandths = 1 hundredth) and multiplying that result by another 10 gives a tenth (10 hundredths = 1 tenth). Multiplying by 10 twice is the same as multiplying by 100.

     1 thousandth x 100 = 1 tenth
     7 thousandths x 100 = 7 tenths
     0.007 x 100 = **0.7**
   - Write an expression such as 1.234×100. Show what happens to the digit in each place value when it is multiplied by 100.

$$\begin{aligned} 1.234 \times 100 &= (1 \times 100) + (0.2 \times 100) + (0.03 \times 100) + (0.004 \times 100) \\ &= 100 + 20 + 3 + 0.4 \\ &= 123.4 \end{aligned}$$

   - Point out that the value of each digit is now 100 times as much, i.e. two place values to the left. As a result, the decimal point is moved 2 places to the right.
   - Discuss **task 8, textbook p. 10.**
   - Discuss **tasks 9-10, textbook p. 11**.
     - Each thousandth, when multiplied by 1000, becomes one whole. This is the same as multiplying it by 10 three times. Similarly, each hundredth becomes a ten.
     - Ask students what would happen to each tenth. Each tenth, now 3 places to the left, becomes a hundred. Moving the decimal point 3 places to the right results in each moving each digit 3 place values to the left.

2. Have students do **task 11, textbook p. 11**.
   - Give students some missing factor problems where they must determine if the missing factor is 10, 100, or 1000, such as the following:
     - $0.034 \times$ _____ $= 0.34$
     - $12.35 \times$ _____ $= 1235$
     - $0.592 \times$ _____ $= 592$

Workbook Exercise 5

Activity 1.2c **Multiply by hundreds and thousands**

1. Discuss multiplying by hundreds and thousands.
   - Write the expression 3.421×3 on the board and ask students to find the answer. Students can use the multiplication algorithm or use mental calculation.

     $3.421 \times 3 = 10.263$
   - Then, write the expression 3.421×30 on the board and ask for a solution. Students should be able to supply the answer by using the previous answer and just moving the decimal point over one place to the right.

     $3.421 \times 30 = 10.263 \times 10 = 102.63$
   - Now, write the expression 3.421×300 on the board and ask for a solution. Since $300 = 3 \times 100$, we can use the first answer and move the decimal over two places.

     $3.421 \times 300 = 10.263 \times 100 = 1026.3$
   - Finally, write the expression 3.421×3000 on the board. Lead students to see that since $3000 = 3 \times 1000$, to find the answer to 3.421×3000, we can use the answer to 3.421×3 and move the decimal point over three places.

     $3.421 \times 3000 = 10.263 \times 1000 = 10{,}263$
   - Point out that we can also multiply first by a hundred or a thousand, and then by the non-zero digit.

     $$\begin{aligned} 3.421 \times 3000 &= 3.421 \times 1000 \times 3 \\ &= 3421 \times 3 \\ &= 10{,}263 \end{aligned}$$
   - Discuss **tasks 12-13, textbook p. 11**.

2. Have students do **task 14, textbook p. 11**.
   - Students can also do **problems 8(a)-8(c), Review A, textbook p. 22**.

Workbook Exercise 6

Part 3: Division by Tens, Hundreds or Thousands — 3 sessions

Objectives

- Divide a decimal number by tens, hundreds, or thousands.

Materials

- Number discs (discs with 0.001, 0.01, 0.1, 1, 10, and 100 written on them)

Homework

- Workbook Exercise 7
- Workbook Exercise 8
- Workbook Exercise 9

Notes

In *Primary Mathematics 4A*, students learned to divide tens, hundreds, and thousands by tens, hundreds, or thousands. Here, the concepts are extended to decimals.

When a whole number with a 0 in the ones place is divided by 10, the 0 in the ones place is removed from the whole number.

$12{,}34\mathbf{0} \div 10 = 1{,}234$

When a decimal or a whole number with a digit other than 0 in the ones place is divided by 10, the decimal point is moved one place to the left, and the value of each digit becomes one tenth of its previous value.

$123\mathbf{4}.5 \div 10 = 123.45$

$\mathbf{0}.2 \div 10 = 0.02$

When a whole number with 0 in both the tens and ones places is divided by 100, two 0's are removed from the whole number.

$12{,}300 \div 100 = 123$

$1234.5 \div 100 = 12.345$

When a decimal number is divided by 100, the decimal point is moved two places to the left. If necessary, one or more 0's are added.

$1.2 \div 100 = 0.012$

After division by 100, the digit in each place value of the decimal number has been moved two places to the right relative to the decimal point, and the value of the digit has become one hundredth (or, a tenth of a tenth) of its previous value.

Similarly, dividing by 1000 involves moving the decimal point three places to the left. This moves each digit three places to the right, making the value of each digit one thousandth of its previous value.

$12{,}000 \div 1000 = 12$

$123 \div 1000 = 0.123$

$2 \div 1000 = 0.002$

Dividing by a ten, hundred, or thousand can be done in two steps. First, we divide by the non-zero digit; and then move the decimal point the appropriate number of places to the left. Or, we can first move the decimal point to the left, and then divide by the non-zero digit.

$$\begin{aligned} 31.2 \div 600 &= 31.2 \div 6 \div 100 \\ &= 5.2 \div 100 \\ &= 0.052 \end{aligned}$$

$$\begin{aligned} 31.2 \div 600 &= 31.2 \div 100 \div 6 \\ &= 0.312 \div 6 \\ &= 0.052 \end{aligned}$$

Activity 1.3a **Divide by tens**

1. Illustrate dividing a decimal number by 10.
   - Refer to **textbook p. 12**. Use number discs to illustrate the process.
   - Guide students to see that each one, when divided by 10, is a tenth.

     1 one ÷ 10 = 1 tenth
     3 ones ÷ 10 = 3 tenths
     $3 \div 10 = 0.3$

   - Each tenth, when divided by 10, is a hundredth.

     1 tenth ÷ 10 = 1 hundredth
     3 tenths ÷ 10 = 3 hundredths
     $0.3 \div 10 = 0.03$

   - Each hundredth, when divided by 10, is a thousandth.

     1 hundredth ÷ 10 = 1 thousandth
     3 hundredths ÷ 10 = 3 thousandths
     $0.03 \div 10 = 0.003$

   - Have students illustrate **task 1, textbook p. 13** with number discs and find the answers, or simply find the answer.
   - Discuss **task 2, textbook p. 13**. Each digit is divided by 10.
   - Discuss **task 3, textbook p. 13**.
     - Students should see that when a decimal number is divided by 10, we move the decimal point one place to the left. This causes the digit in each place to be divided by ten; that is, the digit moves to one place to the right with respect to the decimal point, where its value is now one tenth its original value.

2. Have students do **task 4, textbook p. 13.**

3. Discuss dividing by tens.
   - Write the expression $31.2 \div 4$. Have students solve it mentally (or with division algorithm.)

     $31.2 \div 4 = 7.8$

   - Write the expression $31.2 \div 40$. Lead students to see that we can do the problem in two steps: first divide by 4, and then move the decimal point back one place (divide by 10).

     $$31.2 \div 40 = 31.2 \div 4 \div 10 = 7.8 \div 10 = 0.78$$

4. Have students do **tasks 5-6, textbook p. 14**.

5. Optional: Discuss multiplication by tenths.
   - Write the expression 20×0.1 on the board. Since 0.1 is the same as $\frac{1}{10}$, we can also write this as $20 \times \frac{1}{10}$, or $\frac{20}{10}$, or $20 \div 10$. In effect, we are multiplying by one tenth, and this is the same as dividing by 10; the value of each digit will be one tenth as much. So, by moving the decimal point over one place to the left, we are multiplying by 0.1.

     $$20 \times 0.1 = 20 \times \frac{1}{10} = \frac{20}{10} = 20 \div 10 = 2$$

- Write the expression 2.2×0.1 on the board and ask students to solve it. They can simply move the decimal point one place to the left, as they would do when dividing by 10.

$2.2 \times 0.1 = 0.22$

- Write the expression 234.5×0.1 and ask students for the answer. The value of each digit becomes a tenth as much, since the decimal point has been moved one place to the left.

$234.5 \times 0.1 = 23.45$

- Write the expression 1.1×0.2 and have students solve it. Since 0.2 is equivalent to 2×0.1, this can be solved in two steps. We can multiply 1.1 by 2, and then move the decimal point one place to the left (multiplying each digit by a tenth).

$$\begin{aligned} 1.1 \times 0.2 &= 1.1 \times 2 \times 0.1 \\ &= 2.2 \times 0.1 \\ &= 0.22 \end{aligned}$$

- Point out that although multiplying by 0.1 is the same as dividing by 10, it does not follow that multiplying by 0.2 is the same as dividing by 20. 0.2 is $\frac{2}{10}$, not $\frac{1}{20}$

$$\begin{aligned} 1.1 \times 0.2 &= 1.1 \times \frac{2}{10} \\ &= 1.1 \times 2 \div 10 \end{aligned}$$

- Give students some problems for practice:
  - $30 \times 0.1 = ?$ (3)
  - $30 \times 0.4 = ?$ (12)
  - $40 \times 0.5 = ?$ (20)
  - $145 \times 0.6 = ?$ (87)
  - $4.5 \times 0.6 = ?$ (2.7)
  - $9.6 \times 0.3 = ?$ (2.88)

Workbook Exercise 7

Activity 1.3b **Divide by 100 and 1000**

1. Illustrate dividing a decimal number by 100 and 1000.
   - Refer to **task 7, textbook p. 14**. Illustrate with number discs.
   - Lead students to see that each 1, when divided by 100, is a hundredth. You can show that dividing a one by 10 gives a tenth and dividing that result by another 10 gives a hundredth. Dividing by 10 twice is the same as dividing by 100.

   1 one $\div 100 = 1$ hundredth so
   4 ones $\div 100 = 4$ hundredths
   4 $\div 100 = 0.04$

   - Write an expression such as $123.4 \div 100$. Split it out as follows, discussing each answer with students.

$$\begin{aligned} 123.4 \div 100 &= (100 \div 100) + (20 \div 100) + (3 \div 100) + (0.4 \div 100) \\ &= 1 + 0.2 + 0.03 + 0.004 \\ &= 1.234 \end{aligned}$$

   - Note that each digit in the original number has moved two places to the right. That is, the decimal place has been moved two places to the left.
   - Discuss **task 8, textbook p. 14**.

- Discuss **task 9, textbook p. 15**. Each 1, when divided by 1000, becomes a thousandth. This is the same as dividing it by 10 three times; each digit is moved 3 places to the right.
- Use number discs to illustrate 50 ÷ 1000. Each ten becomes a hundredth, which has moved it 3 places to its (previous) right. Similarly, each hundredth becomes a tenth.

$$5 \div 1000 = 0.005$$
$$50 \div 1000 = 0.05$$
$$500 \div 1000 = 0.5$$

- Now, illustrate 500 ÷ 1000.
- Discuss **task 10, textbook p. 15**.

2. Have students do **task 11, textbook p. 11**.
   - Give students some missing factor problems where they must determine if the missing value is 10, 100, or 1000, such as the following:
     - ➢ $3.4 \div \_\_\_\_\_ = 0.34$
     - ➢ $1235 \div \_\_\_\_\_ = 1.235$
     - ➢ $592 \div \_\_\_\_\_ = 5.92$

Workbook Exercise 8

Activity 1.3c **Divide by hundreds and thousands**

1. Discuss dividing by hundreds and thousands.
   - Write an expression, such as 31.2 ÷ 600. Explain that we can solve this by first dividing by 6 and then by 100. Or, we could first divide by 100 and then by 6.
   - Show how we can do this with the division using the division algorithm. For this we first move the decimal point of both the divisor (600) and of the dividend (31.2) two places to the left, which gives us 0.312 ÷ 6.
   - Point out that another way to do this division is by finding the equivalent fraction, $\frac{31.2}{600}$. We divide both numerator and denominator of this fraction by 100, $\frac{0.312 \times 100}{6 \times 100} = \frac{0.312}{6}$. (This is now the same result as above, 0.312 ÷ 6.) Or, we can simplify our fraction another way, dividing both numerator and denominator by 6 first. $\frac{31.2}{600} = \frac{5.2}{100} = 0.052$.
   - Discuss **tasks 12-13, textbook p. 15**.

$$31.2 \div 600 = 31.2 \div 6 \div 100 = 5.2 \div 100 = 0.052$$

$$31.2 \div 600 = 31.2 \div 100 \div 6 = 0.312 \div 6 = 0.052$$

$$6\,0\,0\overline{)3\,1.2} \qquad 6.0\overline{)0.3\,1\,2} = .0\,5\,2$$

```
      .0 5 2
6.0)0.3 1 2
      3 0
        1 2
        1 2
          0
```

2. Have students do **task 14, textbook p. 15**.
   - Students can also do **problems 8(d)-8(f), Review A, textbook p. 22**.

3. Optional: Discuss multiplication by hundredths. (Do this only if you have already discussed multiplying by tenths in the previous activity).
   - Write the expression 22.3×0.01 on the board. Since 0.01 is the same as $\frac{1}{100}$, we have several ways to write this: $22.3 \times \frac{1}{100}$, $\frac{22.3}{100}$ or $22.3 \div 100$. Multiplying by one hundredth is the same as dividing by 100, changing the value of each digit to one hundredth as much.

     $$\begin{aligned} 22.3 \times 0.01 &= 22.3 \times \frac{1}{100} \\ &= \frac{22.3}{100} \\ &= 22.3 \div 100 \\ &= 0.223 \end{aligned}$$

   - Write the expression 22.3×0.03 and have students solve it. Since 0.03 is equivalent to 3×0.01, this can be solved in two steps. We can multiply 22.3 by 3, and then move the decimal point two places to the left (multiplying the value of each digit by a hundredth).

     $$\begin{aligned} 22.3 \times 0.03 &= 22.3 \times 3 \times 0.01 \\ &= 66.9 \times 0.01 \\ &= 0.669 \end{aligned}$$

   - Point out that although multiplying by 0.01 is the same as dividing by 100, it does not follow that multiplying by 0.3 is the same as dividing by 300. 0.3 is $\frac{3}{100}$, not $\frac{1}{300}$.

     $$\begin{aligned} 22.3 \times 0.3 &= 22.3 \times \frac{3}{100} \\ &= 22.3 \times 3 \div 100 \end{aligned}$$

   - Give students some problems for practice:
     - $400 \times 0.01 = ?$ (4)
     - $40 \times 0.01 = ?$ (0.4)
     - $500 \times 0.04 = ?$ (20)
     - $512 \times 0.04 = ?$ (20.48)
     - $51.2 \times 0.04 = ?$ (2.048)

Workbook Exercise 9

Part 4: Multiplication by a 2-digit Whole Number — 2 sessions

Objectives

- Multiply a decimal number by a 2-digit whole number.
- Estimate the product in multiplication of decimal numbers.

Materials

- Number discs (discs with 0.001, 0.01, 0.1, 1, 10, and 100 written on them)

Homework

- Workbook Exercise 10
- Workbook Exercise 11

Notes

In *Primary Mathematics 4A*, students learned to multiply a whole number by a 2-digit whole number. This was reviewed in *Primary Mathematics 5A*. Here, the skill is extended to multiplication of a decimal number by a 2 digit whole number.

Multiplication by 2 digit numbers is done in three steps — multiplying by the tens, then multiplying by the ones, and then adding the products. The problem can be written vertically so that the places can be aligned, which makes it easier to keep correct track of the place values. While the 0 resulting from multiplying by the tens digit can be left out, encourage students to include it.

$$
\begin{aligned}
567 \times 52 &= (567 \times 50) + (567 \times 2) \\
&= (567 \times 5 \times 10) + (567 \times 2) \\
&= (2835 \times 10) + 1134 \\
&= 28{,}350 + 1134 \\
&= 29{,}484
\end{aligned}
$$

$$
\begin{array}{rrl}
 & 567 & \\
\times & 52 & \\
\hline
 & 1134 & = 567 \times 2 \\
 & 28350 & = 567 \times 50 \\
\hline
 & 29484 &
\end{array}
$$

Note that when multiplying in the vertical format, by tradition we multiply first by the ones and then by the tens. This helps students align their columns correctly by placing a 0 below the ones to indicate that the answer is tens. $5\ \textit{tens} \times 567 = 2835\ \textit{tens}$

Multiplication of a decimal number by a 2-digit whole number is a similar process. Traditionally, the decimal is not written into the partial products, but instead is put in place into the answer, which is the sum of the partial products.

$$
\begin{aligned}
5.67 \times 52 &= (5.67 \times 50) + (5.67 \times 2) \\
&= (5.67 \times 5 \times 10) + (5.67 \times 2) \\
&= (28.35 \times 10) + 11.34 \\
&= 283.50 + 11.34 \\
&= 294.84
\end{aligned}
$$

$$
\begin{array}{rrl}
 & 5.67 & \\
\times & 52 & \\
\hline
 & 1134 & = 5.67 \times 2 \\
 & 28350 & = 5.67 \times 50 \\
\hline
 & 294.84 &
\end{array}
$$

As a check, students should estimate answers in advance of carrying out calculations. This is especially important for multiplication or division problems, where careless digit alignment often causes place value error.

$$5.67 \times 52 \approx 6 \times 50 = 300$$

Activity 1.4a **Multiply a decimal number by a 2-digit number**

1. Discuss multiplying a decimal number by a 2-digit whole number.
   - Write a relatively simple multiplication problem of a decimal number by a 2-digit whole number, such as 2.2×21.
   - Have students estimate the answer. They should round both numbers so that each has only one non-zero digit.

     $$2.2 \times 21 \approx 2 \times 20 = 40$$

   - Next, show students that we can split 21 into tens and ones and multiply each part by 2.2.

     $$\begin{aligned} 2.2 \times 21 &= (2.2 \times 20) + (2.2 \times 1) \\ &= 44 + 2.2 \\ &= 46.2 \end{aligned}$$

   - Show the same problem worked vertically, multiplying first the ones and then the tens.
   - Point out that when multiplying by the ten, (2.2×2 tens) the product is one place value more over to the left than it would be when multiplying by 2. Put a 0 in the ones place to keep track of where the digits should go.

     $$\begin{array}{r} 2.2 \\ \times \quad \underline{2\,1} \\ 2.2 \\ \underline{4\,4.0} \\ 4\,6.2 \end{array}$$

   - Because one factor is actually a tenth of 22, the final product will also be a tenth of 22×21. We can work the problem the same way as if we were multiplying 22×21, and write in the decimal point at the end, into the answer. Tell them that this is the traditional way of showing the calculation.

     $$\begin{array}{r} 2.2 \\ \times \quad \underline{2\,1} \\ 2\,2 \\ \underline{4\,4} \\ 4\,6.2 \end{array}$$

   - Point out that if we do not align the digits correctly in the multiplication process, the result will differ from the estimate in place value. Estimating the answer helps catch such errors.

     $$\begin{array}{r} 2.2 \\ \times \quad \underline{2\,1} \\ 2\,2 \\ \underline{4\,4} \\ 6.6 \end{array} \quad \times$$

   - Repeat with a number where multiplying by the ones will lead to a 0 in the lowest place value, such as 2.22×25. Have students estimate the answer before carrying out the calculations.

     $$2.22 \times 25 \approx 2 \times 30 = 60$$

   - The answer has a 0 at the end in the hundredths place. Customarily this final 0 can be left off as it does not change the value of the number. $55.5 = 55.50$

     $$\begin{aligned} 2.22 \times 25 & \\ &= (2.22 \times 20) + (2.22 \times 5) \\ &= (2.22 \times 2 \times 10) + (2.22 \times 5) \\ &= (4.44 \times 10) + 11.10 \\ &= 44.4 + 11.1 \\ &= 55.5 \end{aligned}$$

   - Estimating the answer first will warn us if we then make a mistake with place value in the calculation.

     $$\begin{array}{rl} 2.2\,2 & \\ \times \quad \underline{2\,5} & \\ 1\,1.1\,0 & \leftarrow 2.22 \times 5 \\ \underline{4\,4.4\,0} & \leftarrow 2.22 \times 20 \\ 5\,5.5\,0 & \end{array}$$

   - Discuss the problems in the **textbook, p. 16**. The second problem is done the same way as the first, and then the decimal point is put in. Estimating first helps us to know we have aligned the digits correctly and put the decimal point in the correct place.

2. Have students do **task 1, textbook p. 17**.
   Have them also find the actual products. (91,476; 9147.6; 914.76)

   Workbook Exercise 10
   Workbook Exercise 11 (part of #1)
   Since multiplication by a 2-digit number is often a long process for students, and since exercise 10 is relatively short, you may also want to assign part of exercise 11 at this time.)

Activity 1.4b **Multiply a decimal number by a 2-digit whole number**

1. Discuss **task 2, textbook p. 17**.
   - Go over the estimate shown in (a). Then tell students that in this problem, since 0.23 is less than 1, they can immediately see the answer has to be less than the 59.
   - Then discuss the steps in (b).

2. Have students do **task 3, textbook p. 17**.

3. Optional: Discuss multiplying a decimal by a decimal.
   - Refer back to **task 2, textbook p. 17** and vary it. Ask students what they think the answer would be for 0.23×5.9.
   - 0.23×59 was solved the same way as 23×59, with the decimal point in the final answer moving two places to the left (since 0.23 is a hundredth as much as 23). This time, the multiplication is again the same but the decimal point in the final answer is moved to the left by the number of places in *both* factors. First, left two places for the factor 0.23, and then left one more place for the other factor, 5.9 (5.9 is a tenth as much as 59).
   - Provide additional examples.

$$\begin{array}{r} 0.23 \\ \times \quad 5.9 \\ \hline 207 \\ 1150 \\ \hline 1.357 \end{array}$$

   Workbook Exercise 11

Part 5: Conversion of Measurements — 4 sessions

Objectives

- Convert a measurement in decimal numbers to a smaller unit or to a compound unit.
- Convert a measurement to a larger measurement unit where the answer is a decimal number.

Materials

- Number discs (discs with 0.001, 0.01, 0.1, 1, 10, and 100 written on them)

Homework

- Workbook Exercise 12
- Workbook Exercise 13
- Workbook Exercise 14

Notes

In *Primary Mathematics 5A*, students learned to convert measurements involving fractions. In this section, they will learn to convert measures involving decimals.

Students need to be familiar with conversion units – how many smaller units equal a larger unit (e.g., 100 cm = 1 m, 12 in. = 1 ft).

To convert a measurement in a larger unit to a smaller unit, *multiply* by the conversion factor. (Each larger unit is made up pf many smaller units.)

1 kg = 1000 g
2 kg = 2 × 1000 g
0.2 kg = 0.2 × 1000 g = 200 g

To convert a measurement in a smaller unit to a larger unit, *divide* by the conversion factor. The smaller unit is "merged" into a larger unit, so there are fewer larger units for the same length, width, or volume. The division of small units into larger ones can be represented as a fraction.

$$1\text{ g} = \frac{1}{1000}\text{ kg}$$

$$2\text{ g} = 2 \times \frac{1}{1000}\text{ kg} = \frac{2}{1000}\text{ kg} = 0.002\text{ kg}$$

In the metric system, all of the multiplication and division in this section will be by 100 (meter to centimeter) or 1000 (kilogram to gram, kilometer to meter, liter to milliliter) so the student can multiply mentally by moving the decimal point over 2 or 3 places.

US edition:

For US students more used to standard U.S. measurement, a main cause of error will be remembering that 1 m is 100 cm, not 1000 cm. (1 liter = 1000 ml, 1 km = 1000 m, 1 kg = 1000 g)

Standard U.S. measurements are usually given as fractions, rather than as decimals. However, the concepts in converting standard U.S. measurements expressed in decimals to smaller units are the same.

To convert to a smaller unit, we multiply by the conversion factor. To convert to a larger unit, we divide by the conversion factor.

$1 \text{ ft} = 12 \text{ in.}$
$2 \text{ ft} = 2 \times 12 \text{ in.} = 24 \text{ in.}$
$0.5 \text{ ft} = 0.5 \times 12 \text{ in.} = 6 \text{ in.}$

All of the answers in this section will be whole numbers. So for US standard measurements, the decimal numbers will be 0.25, 0.5, or 0.75. It is easier to find $\frac{1}{4}$ of 12 or even $\frac{3}{4}$ of 12 than it is to multiply 0.25×12 or 0.75×12. So, when converting U.S. measurements, the student can convert the decimal to a fraction first.

$1 \text{ in.} = \frac{1}{12} \text{ ft}$

$$\begin{aligned} 9 \text{ in.} &= 9 \times \frac{1}{12} \text{ ft} \\ &= \frac{9}{12} \text{ ft} \\ &= \frac{3}{4} \text{ ft} \\ &= 0.75 \text{ ft} \end{aligned}$$

$0.5 \text{ ft} = \frac{1}{2} \times 12 \text{ in.} = 6 \text{ in.}$

Sometimes it is easier to deal with decimals, as with metric measurements which are based on the decimal system, and sometimes it is easier to deal with fractions. But any decimal can be made into a fraction, just by using the right power of 10; as in $37.4 = \frac{374}{10}$, or in $3.74 = \frac{374}{100}$.

Activity 1.5a **Convert a measurement to a smaller unit**

1. Review the conversion factors for measurements.
   - A partial list of conversion units is given on **p. 19 of the textbook**.
   - US: Besides what is on that list, ask for the number of half-gallons in a gallon (2), the number of quarts in a half-gallon (2), the number of inches in a yard (36 in.) and the number of cups in a gallon (16 c).
   - Ask students how they would convert a whole-number measurement into a smaller unit. For example, ask how they would find the number of centimeters in 10 meters. They should remember that to convert to a smaller measurement unit, we *multiply* by the conversion factor.

2. Discuss conversion of a decimal-number measurement to a smaller measurement unit for the metric system.
   - Draw a bar on the board and label it 1 meter. Ask students for the number of centimeters in the meter. (100)
   - Mark a point about one fifth of the way and mark the length as 0.2. Ask student how long the part is in centimeters. They may see that 0.2 is a fifth of a meter, and so is a fifth of 100, or 20 cm.
   - Tell them we can find the number of centimeters in 0.2 m by multiplying it by 100, the number of centimeters in a meter. Write the equation.
   - Write 2.2 m and ask students how many centimeters are in 2.2 m. Lead them to see that we can also multiply 2.2 m by 100 to get the answer. 2.2 m is 2.2 of 100 cm.
   - Ask students to express 2.2 m in compound units of both meters and centimeters. For this, the whole-number part does not change; only the decimal part is converted.

1 m

0.2 m

$$0.2 \text{ m} = 0.2 \times 100 \text{ cm} = 20 \text{ cm}$$

$$2.2 \text{ m} = 2.2 \times 100 \text{ cm} = 220 \text{ cm}$$

$$2.2 \text{ m} = 2 \text{ m } 20 \text{ cm}$$

3. Discuss **textbook p. 18**.

4. US: Discuss conversion of a decimal-number measurement to a smaller measurement unit for the U.S. standard system.
   - Draw a bar representing 1 ft. Mark a length one fourth of the way along the bar and label it as 0.25 ft. Ask students how many inches are in a foot. (12) Then ask them for the number of inches in 0.25 ft. Students may realize that 0.25 is a fourth, and a fourth of a foot is 3 inches.
   - Tell students that we can find the number of inches in 0.25 ft by multiplying 0.25 by the number of inches in a foot, 12.
   - Have students find the number of inches in 2.25 ft. We can multiply 2.25 by 12 to find the number of inches.
   - Have students express the answer in compound units. We multiply only the decimal portion.
   - Re-do the earlier conversion equations using fractions instead. Point out that with U.S. measurements it may be easier to do the calculations with fractions rather than with decimals.

$$0.25 \text{ ft} = 0.25 \times 12 \text{ in.} = 3 \text{ in.}$$

$$2.25 \text{ ft} = 2.25 \times 12 \text{ in.} = 27 \text{ in.}$$

$$2.25 \text{ ft} = 2 \text{ ft } 3 \text{ in.}$$

$$0.25 \text{ ft} = \frac{1}{4} \times 12 \text{ in.} = 3 \text{ in.}$$

$$2.25 \text{ ft.} = 2\frac{1}{4} \times 12 \text{ in.} = \frac{9}{\cancel{4}_1} \times \cancel{12}^3 = 27 \text{ in.}$$

- Students should memorize the math facts shown at the right, if they have not already done so.
- Ask students to supply the answers to the following:
  - ➢ 0.25 ft = _____ in. (3)
  - ➢ 0.5 ft = _____ in. (6)
  - ➢ 0.75 ft = _____ in. (9)
  - ➢ 0.25 lb = _____ oz (4)
  - ➢ 0.5 lb = _____ oz (8)
  - ➢ 0.75 lb = _____ oz (12)

$0.25 = \frac{1}{4}$

$0.5 = \frac{1}{2}$

$0.75 = \frac{3}{4}$

$\frac{1}{4} \times 12 = 3$

$\frac{1}{2} \times 12 = 6$

$\frac{3}{4} \times 12 = 9$

$\frac{1}{4} \times 16 = 4$

$\frac{1}{2} \times 16 = 8$

$\frac{3}{4} \times 16 = 12$

5. Discuss **tasks 1-2** and **4, textbook p. 19**.

6. Have students do **tasks 3** and **5, textbook p. 19**.

   Workbook Exercise 12

Activity 1.5b **Convert a measurement to a larger unit**

1. Discuss conversion of a measurement to a larger measurement unit for the metric system.
   - Draw a bar on the board and divide it into 10 units. Tell students that you are going to measure a line with this bar. Draw a line above it 7 units long.
   - Ask students for the length of the line compared to the total length. They may say that the line is $\frac{7}{10}$ of the total bar.

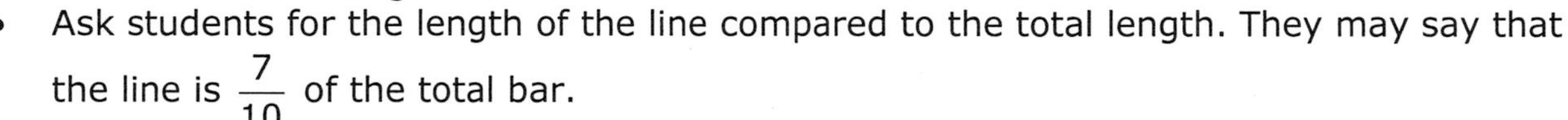

   - Point out that since we know that 10 units = 1 bar, then a line that is 7 units long is $\frac{7}{10}$ of the total bar. We can also say its length is 0.7 of the total bar.
   - Write 70 cm. Ask students "70 cm is what fraction of a meter?" To find this, we write the part (70) over the total in the same units (100 cm).

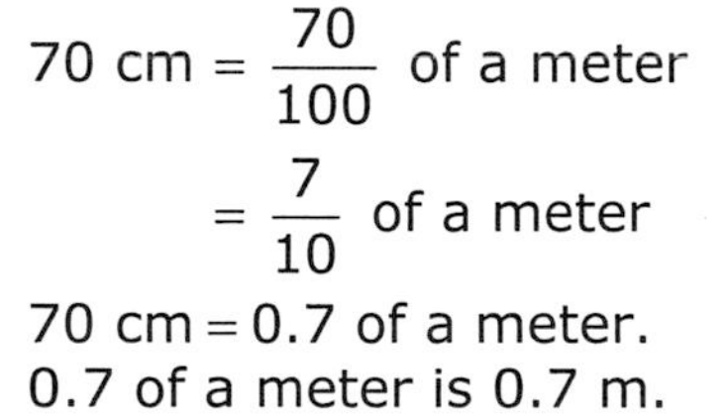

$70 \text{ cm} = \frac{70}{100}$ of a meter

$= \frac{7}{10}$ of a meter

   - Ask students to convert this fraction to a decimal. 70 cm is 0.7 of a meter, or 0.7 m.

70 cm = 0.7 of a meter.
0.7 of a meter is 0.7 m.

   - So, if we have a measurement in a small unit, we can find the length in terms of a larger unit by *dividing* by the conversion unit, or writing it as a fraction of the larger unit and then changing that into a decimal.
   - Ask students for 50 m in kilometers.

$50 \text{ m} = \frac{50}{1000} \text{ km}$
$= 0.05 \text{ km}$

   - Ask students for 1 km 50 m in kilometers. We only have to convert the 50 m.

$1 \text{ km } 50 \text{ m} = 1 \text{ km} + 0.05 \text{ km}$
$= 1.05 \text{ km}$

2. Discuss tasks **6** and **9**, **textbook p. 20**.

3. Have students do tasks **7** and **8**, **textbook p. 20**.

4. US: Discuss conversion of a measurement to a larger measurement unit for the U.S. standard system.

   - Draw a line on the board and label it as 9 in. long. Ask students, "9 in. is what fraction of a foot?" To find this, students must first convert the foot to inches.
   - Then ask them to express that fraction as a decimal.
   - Point out that to find out what smaller unit of measurement is in a larger unit, we divide by the conversion factor.

$$\begin{aligned} 9 \text{ in.} &= \frac{9}{12} \text{ of a foot} \\ &= \frac{3}{4} \text{ of a foot} \\ &= 0.75 \text{ ft} \end{aligned}$$

   - Ask students to find 4 oz in pounds.

$$\begin{aligned} 4 \text{ oz} &= \frac{4}{16} \text{ lb} \\ &= \frac{1}{4} \text{ lb} \\ &= 0.25 \text{ lb} \end{aligned}$$

5. Have students do task **10**, **textbook p. 20**.

   Workbook Exercise 13

Activity 1.5c **Convert a measurement to a larger unit**

1. Discuss **task 11, textbook p. 20**.
   - Two methods are shown here for converting a metric measurement to a larger unit when the value of the measurement is greater than the conversion factor.
   - In method 1, we split the value into two parts; the multiple of the conversion factor, and the remainder. Students learned to do this in *Primary Mathematics 4A*, finding the remainder as a fraction of the larger unit. Here, they need to find the remainder as a decimal number.
   - In method 2, we divide the whole value by the conversion factor. This results in an improper fraction which can directly be converted into a decimal number. Since we are dividing by 100 or 1000, this just involves correct placement of the decimal point.

$$\begin{aligned} 3080 \text{ g} &= 3000 \text{ g} + 80 \text{ g} \\ &= 3 \text{ kg} + \frac{80}{1000} \text{ kg} \\ &= 3 \text{ kg} + .08 \text{ kg} \\ &= 3.08 \text{ kg} \end{aligned}$$

$$\begin{aligned} 3080 \text{ g} &= \frac{3080}{1000} \text{ kg} \\ &= 3.08 \text{ kg} \end{aligned}$$

2. US: Discuss converting U.S. standard measurement.
   - Ask students to express 201 inches in feet.
     - Method 1: Divide by the conversion factor.

       201 in. $= 201 \div 12$ ft $= 16.75$ ft

$$
\begin{array}{r}
16.75 \\
12\overline{)201.00} \\
\underline{12} \\
81 \\
\underline{72} \\
9\,0 \\
\underline{8\,4} \\
60 \\
\underline{60} \\
0
\end{array}
$$

     - Method 2: Express inches as a fraction of a foot and simplify the fraction before dividing.

$$
\begin{aligned}
201 \text{ in.} &= \frac{201}{12} \text{ ft} \\
&= \frac{67}{4} \text{ ft} \\
&= 16.75 \text{ ft}
\end{aligned}
$$

     - Method 3: Express inches as a fraction of a foot, then express that as a mixed number, then find the decimal number of the fractional part.

$$
\begin{aligned}
201 \text{ in.} &= \frac{201}{12} \text{ ft} \\
&= \frac{67}{4} \text{ ft} \\
&= 16\frac{3}{4} \text{ ft} \\
&= 16.75 \text{ ft}
\end{aligned}
$$

   - The last two methods are essentially the same. Ask students which method they prefer. Students will probably realize that simplifying the fraction first, when that is possible, will make the division simpler.

3. Have students do **task 12, textbook p. 20**.
   Students can also do **problem 11, Review A, textbook p. 23**.

   Workbook Exercise 14

Activity 1.5d **Practice**

1. Have students do the problems in **Practice 1A, textbook p. 21** and share their answers.
   - You may want to do the (a) part of each question as a class, and then let students work individually.
   - You may want to have students draw models for problems 13 and 14, although most students should be able to solve these even without a diagram.

Review A

Objectives

- Review all topics.

Suggested number of sessions: 2

	Objectives	Textbook	Workbook	Activities
Review A				**2 sessions**
17 18	▪ Review.	pp. 22-24, Review A	Review 1	R.a

Activity R.a **Review**

1. Have students do any problems in **Review A, textbook pp. 22-24.**
   - Students should share their solutions, particularly for the word problems. Possible solutions for some of the problems are shown here.
   - You may also want to have students share their solutions to problems 23-26 in the **Workbook Review 1**. Possible solutions to these are also shown here.
   - You may want to omit problem 24 on p. 24 of the textbook and save it for the beginning of Unit 6 as a review of angle properties of intersecting lines.

Textbook Review A

15. Cost of apples

Cost of pears

1 unit = cost of apples
Each pear unit is 2 apple units, so the cost of pears is 16 units.
Total number of units = 10 + 16 = 26
Total cost = $0.35 × 26 = $9.10
Or:
1 pear = 2 × $0.35 = $0.70
8 pears = 8 × $0.70 = $5.60
10 apples = 10 × $0.35 = $3.50
Total cost = $5.60 + $3.50 = $9.10

16.

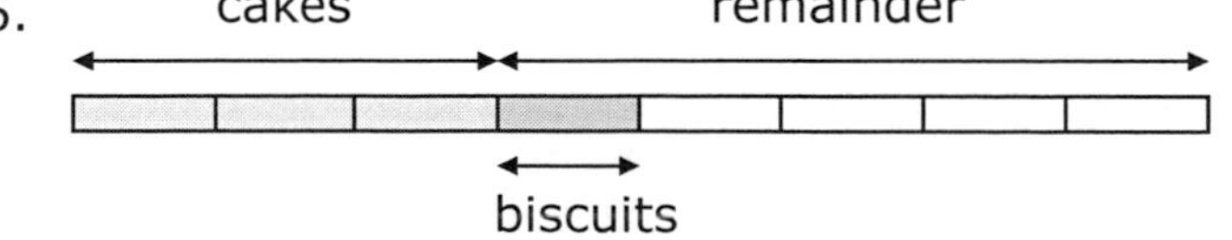

$\frac{1}{5}$ of the remainder is 1 unit. She used 4 units altogether, which is $\frac{1}{2}$ of the flour.

Or: $\frac{3}{8} + \left(\frac{1}{5} \times \frac{5}{8}\right) = \frac{3}{8} + \frac{1}{8} = \frac{4}{8} = \frac{1}{2}$

18. The solution involves finding equivalent fractions of $\frac{1}{3}$ (for the morning) and $\frac{1}{4}$ (for the afternoon) with the same denominator (12). Divide the bar into 12 units.

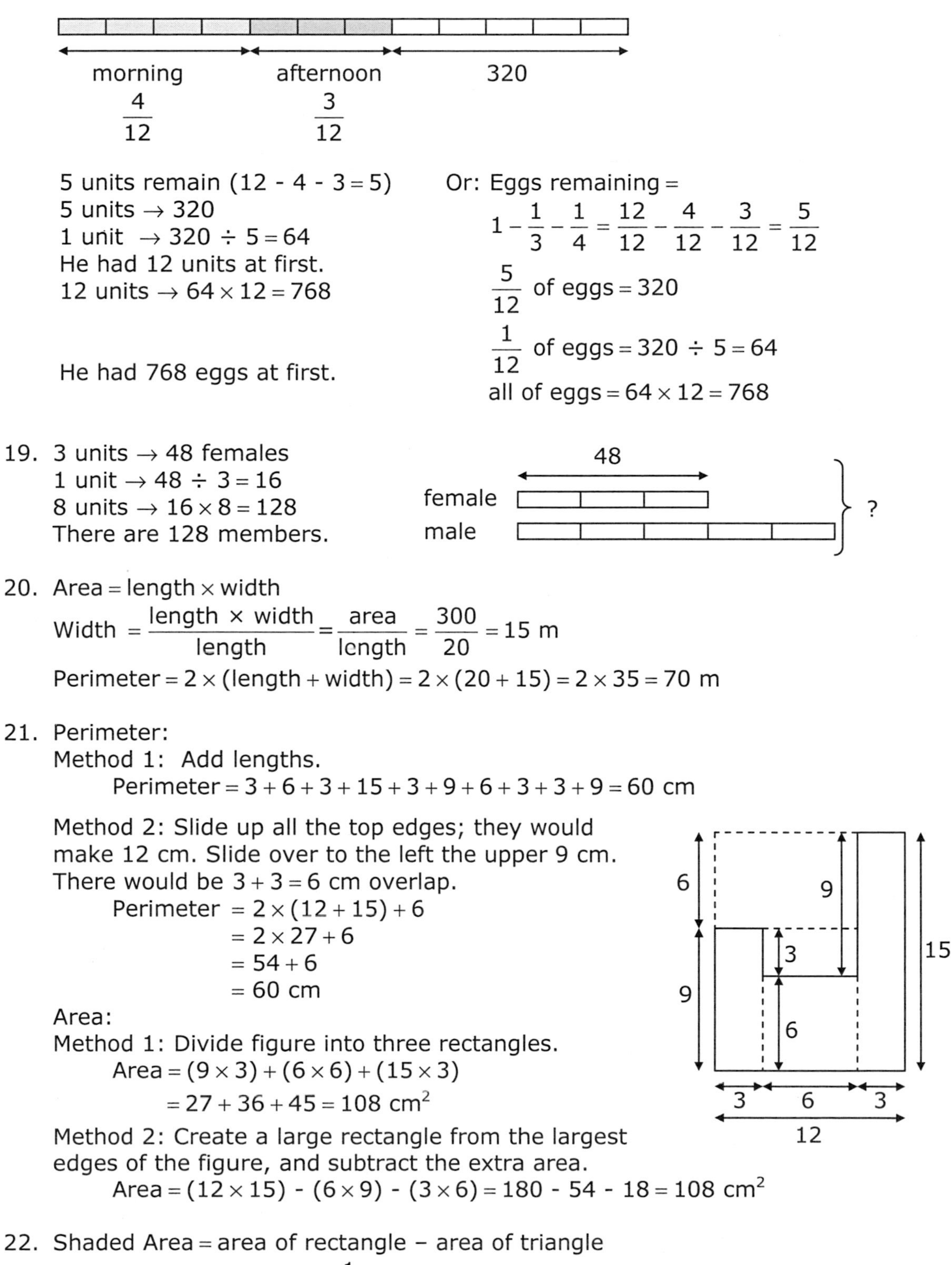

5 units remain $(12 - 4 - 3 = 5)$
5 units $\rightarrow$ 320
1 unit $\rightarrow 320 \div 5 = 64$
He had 12 units at first.
12 units $\rightarrow 64 \times 12 = 768$

He had 768 eggs at first.

Or: Eggs remaining =

$$1 - \frac{1}{3} - \frac{1}{4} = \frac{12}{12} - \frac{4}{12} - \frac{3}{12} = \frac{5}{12}$$

$\frac{5}{12}$ of eggs $= 320$

$\frac{1}{12}$ of eggs $= 320 \div 5 = 64$

all of eggs $= 64 \times 12 = 768$

19. 3 units $\rightarrow$ 48 females
1 unit $\rightarrow 48 \div 3 = 16$
8 units $\rightarrow 16 \times 8 = 128$
There are 128 members.

20. Area = length $\times$ width

$$\text{Width} = \frac{\text{length} \times \text{width}}{\text{length}} = \frac{\text{area}}{\text{length}} = \frac{300}{20} = 15 \text{ m}$$

Perimeter $= 2 \times (\text{length} + \text{width}) = 2 \times (20 + 15) = 2 \times 35 = 70$ m

21. Perimeter:
Method 1: Add lengths.
Perimeter $= 3 + 6 + 3 + 15 + 3 + 9 + 6 + 3 + 3 + 9 = 60$ cm

Method 2: Slide up all the top edges; they would make 12 cm. Slide over to the left the upper 9 cm. There would be $3 + 3 = 6$ cm overlap.

$$\begin{aligned} \text{Perimeter} &= 2 \times (12 + 15) + 6 \\ &= 2 \times 27 + 6 \\ &= 54 + 6 \\ &= 60 \text{ cm} \end{aligned}$$

Area:
Method 1: Divide figure into three rectangles.

$$\begin{aligned} \text{Area} &= (9 \times 3) + (6 \times 6) + (15 \times 3) \\ &= 27 + 36 + 45 = 108 \text{ cm}^2 \end{aligned}$$

Method 2: Create a large rectangle from the largest edges of the figure, and subtract the extra area.

Area $= (12 \times 15) - (6 \times 9) - (3 \times 6) = 180 - 54 - 18 = 108 \text{ cm}^2$

22. Shaded Area = area of rectangle − area of triangle

$$= (10 \times 8) - (\frac{1}{2} \times 10 \times 3) = 80 - 15 = 65 \text{ cm}^2$$

23. A base of the top triangle is 6 cm and the corresponding height is 2 cm.
A base of the bottom triangle is 6 cm and its corresponding height is 6 cm.
Area $= (\frac{1}{2} \times 6 \times 2) + (\frac{1}{2} \times 6 \times 6) = 6 + 18 = 24$ cm^2

Workbook Review 1

23.
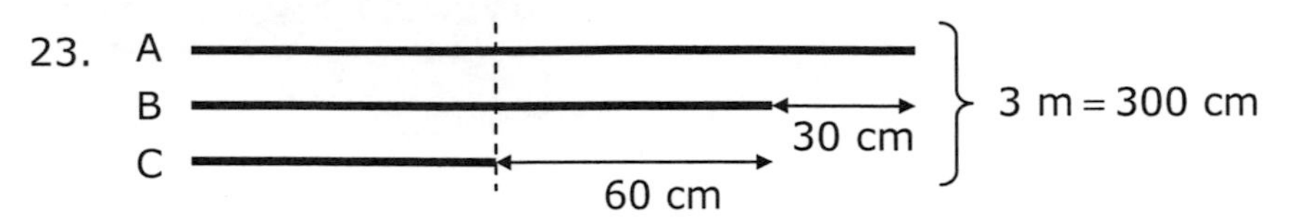

If 30 cm is removed from A, and 60 cm from both A and B, then there will be three lengths equivalent to the length of C. Let the length of C be a unit.
3 units $= 300$ cm - 30 cm - $(2 \times 60$ cm$) = 300 - 30 - 120 = 150$ cm
1 unit $= 150 \div 3 = 50$ cm
String C is 50 cm long.

24.
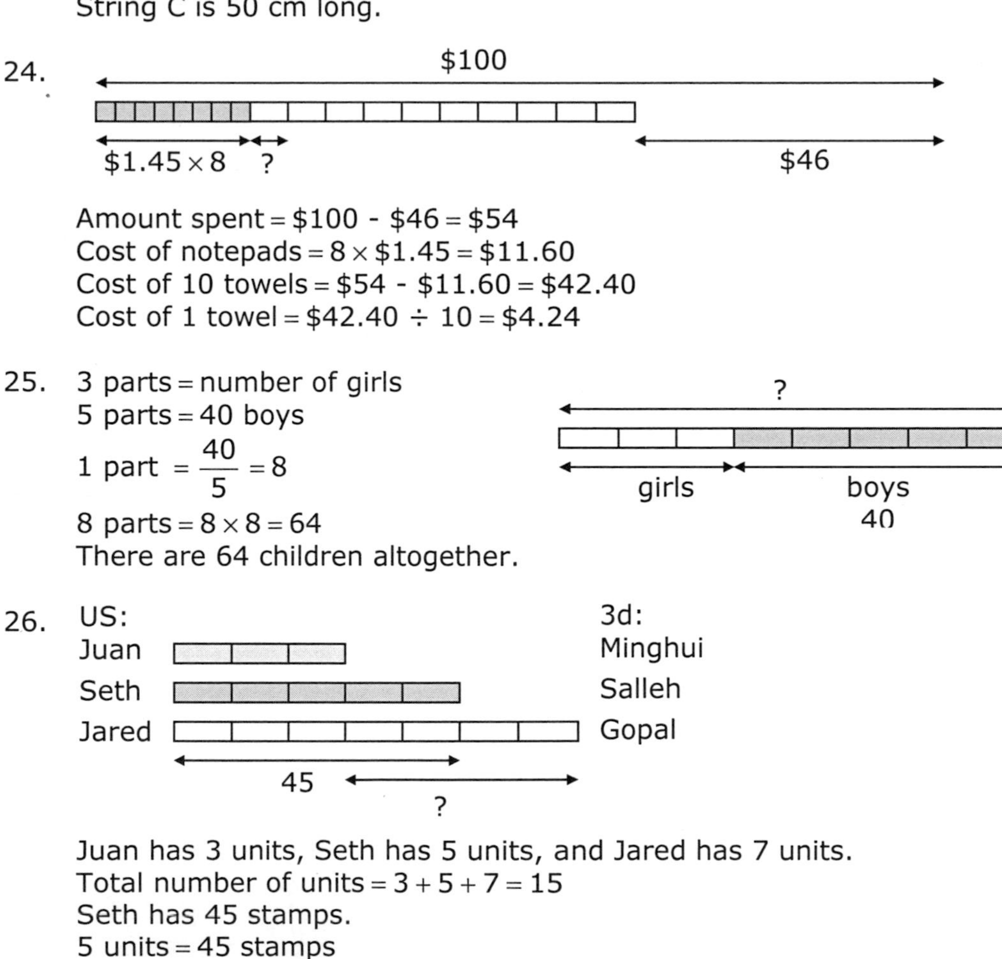

Amount spent $= \$100 - \$46 = \$54$
Cost of notepads $= 8 \times \$1.45 = \$11.60$
Cost of 10 towels $= \$54 - \$11.60 = \$42.40$
Cost of 1 towel $= \$42.40 \div 10 = \$4.24$

25. 3 parts = number of girls
5 parts = 40 boys
1 part $= \frac{40}{5} = 8$
8 parts $= 8 \times 8 = 64$
There are 64 children altogether.

26. US: Juan, Seth, Jared — 3d: Minghui, Salleh, Gopal

Juan has 3 units, Seth has 5 units, and Jared has 7 units.
Total number of units $= 3 + 5 + 7 = 15$
Seth has 45 stamps.
5 units = 45 stamps
1 unit $= 45 \div 5 = 9$ stamps
Jared has 4 more units than Juan.
4 units $= 4 \times 9 = 36$
Jared has 36 more stamps than Juan.

Unit 2 – Percentage

Objectives

- Understand percentage.
- Express a fraction as a percentage.
- Express a decimal number as a percentage.
- Express a percentage as a decimal.
- Express a percentage as a fraction in its simplest form.
- Find the value for a percentage of a whole.
- Solve 1-step and 2-step word problems involving percentage.

Suggested number of sessions: 10

	Objectives	Textbook	Workbook	Activities
Part 1 : Percent				**3 sessions**
19	▪ Understand percentage. ▪ Express a fraction with a denominator of 10 or 100 as a percentage.	p. 25 p. 26, tasks 1-4	Ex. 15	2.1a
20	▪ Express a decimal number as a percentage. ▪ Express a percentage as a decimal number.	p. 27, tasks 5-8	Ex. 16	2.1b
21	▪ Express a percentage as a fraction in its simplest form.	p. 27, tasks 9-10 p. 32, Practice 2A, 2-4	Ex. 17	2.1c
Part 2 : Writing Fractions as Percentages				**3 sessions**
22	▪ Express a fraction as a percentage.	p. 28 p. 29, tasks 1-4 p. 32, Practice 2A, 5,6,11	Ex. 18	2.2a
23	▪ Express a fraction with a denominator that is a multiple of 100 as a percentage.	p. 30, tasks 5-7 p. 32, Practice 2A, 1	Ex. 19	2.2b
24	▪ Solve word problems which involve finding the percentage for a part of the whole.	p. 31, tasks 8-11 p. 32, Practice 2A, 8-13	Ex. 20	2.2c
Part 3 : Percentage of a Quantity				**4 sessions**
25	▪ Find the value for a percentage part when given the whole.	p. 33 p. 34, tasks 1-3 p. 37, Practice 2B, 1	Ex. 21	2.3a
26	▪ Solve word problems which involve finding the value for a percentage part of a whole.	pp. 34-35, tasks 4-5 p. 37, Practice 2B, 2-7	Ex. 22	2.3b
27	▪ Solve word problems which involve interest rates or percent discounts.	pp. 35-36, tasks 6-7 p. 37, Practice 2B, 8-10	Ex. 23	2.3c
28	▪ Solve word problems which involve percent decrease or increase.	p. 36, tasks 8-9 p. 37, Practice 2B, 11-13	Ex. 24	2.3d

Part 1: Percent — 3 sessions

Objectives

- Read and interpret percentage of a whole.
- Express a fraction with a denominator of 10 or 100 as a percentage.
- Express a decimal as a percentage.
- Express a percentage as a decimal.
- Express a percentage as a fraction in its simplest form.

Materials

- 10×10 grids
- Displayable 10x10 grids

Homework

- Workbook Exercise 15
- Workbook Exercise 16
- Workbook Exercise 17

Notes

In this section, students will learn the meaning of percentage. Students have already learned to express parts of a whole as a fraction. Here they will learn to express parts of a whole as a percentage. They will also learn to convert a decimal number to a percentage. Only percentages under 100% will be studied at this level.

The symbol % is read as **percent** and comes from the Latin phrase *per centum*, which means "out of a hundred". The % symbol means "per hundred" or "out of 100". Students might recognize *cent* as representing 100, from *cent*s in a dollar or *cent*imeters in a meter.

One percent (1%) is the same as $\frac{1}{100}$ of a whole.

A fraction with 100 in the denominator can be expressed as a percentage by simply taking the numerator and putting a percent sign after it.

$$\frac{15}{100} = 15\%$$

A fraction with 10 in the denominator can be expressed as a percentage by multiplying its numerator by 10 and putting a percent sign after it.

$$\frac{7}{10} = \frac{70}{100} = 70\%$$

To write a decimal number as a percentage, we can write it as a fraction with denominator of 100, and then write that fraction as a percentage.

$$0.25 = \frac{25}{100} = 25\%$$

$$0.3 = \frac{30}{100} = 30\%$$

To express a percentage as a decimal number, we can first write it as a fraction with a denominator of 100, and then write that fraction as a decimal.

$$25\% = \frac{25}{100} = 0.25$$

To express a percentage as a fraction in its simplest form, we can write it as a fraction with a denominator of 100, and then simplify that fraction.

$$25\% = \frac{25}{100} = \frac{1}{4}$$

Activity 2.1a **Percent**

1. Introduce percentage.
   - Discuss **p. 25 in the textbook**.
   - Students should see that there are 100 seats, and 55 of them are occupied.
   - Tell students that we can write 55 out of 100 as a fraction of 100, or $\frac{55}{100}$.

     55 out of 100 = $\frac{55}{100}$ = 55%

     55% of the seats are occupied.
   - Tell them that there is a special way to write fractions of 100. We can write 55 out of 100 as 55%. The % symbol means "out of 100".
   - Ask students how many seats are unoccupied. Then, ask them what percent of the seats are unoccupied.

     45% of the seats are unoccupied.
   - Write a few more percentages, and ask students what they mean. For example, 25% means 25 out of 100. 100% means 100 out of 100. 100 out of 100 is all of it, so 100 out of 100 is the same as 1 whole.

     25% = 25 out of 100

     100% = 1 whole
   - Ask students for instances where they may have seen percentage. For example, they may have seen a 30% off sale. This would mean that the price has been reduced 30 cents for every 100 cents, i.e., for every dollar.

2. Illustrate percentage with a 10×10 grid.
   - Show students a 10×10 grid. Ask them how many total squares it has.
   - Color in some squares and ask them how many are colored.
   - Ask them what percentage of the whole is colored.
   - Ask them what percentage of the whole is not colored.
   - Discuss **tasks 1-2, textbook p. 26**.
     - Ask students to write the answers first as a percentage, then as a fraction of 100, and then as a fraction in its simplest form.
     - Point out that for 2.(d), 100% of the squares are colored, which is the same as the entire amount, or the whole.
     - Refer to 2.(b). Ask students how many squares there are in one row, and what fraction that is of the whole. ($\frac{1}{10}$). Ask how much of the whole is shaded as a fraction of 10. ($\frac{5}{10}$). So we can express $\frac{5}{10}$ as a percentage by converting it to the equivalent fraction $\frac{50}{100}$, which is the same as 50%.
   - Provide students with square grids and have them do **task 3, textbook p. 26**.
     - Ask students to also write the answers as a fraction out of 100, and as a fraction in its simplest form.

3. Have students do **task 4, textbook p. 26**.
   - You can also ask students to write each fraction in its simplest form. Students will eventually memorize fraction equivalents for some percentages, such as $\frac{3}{4}$ = 75%.

Workbook Exercise 15

Activity 2.1b **Percent and decimal**

1. Discuss expressing a decimal number as a percentage.
   - Write the decimal number 0.55 on the board.
   - Ask students to write it as a fraction, then as a percent.
   - Tell students that although we normally think of the value of a two-place decimal number as a hundredth of 1, a decimal number can also be used with a different whole.
     - Refer back to p. 25 in the textbook. Tell students that we said that 55 out of 100, or $\frac{55}{100}$, or 55% of the total seats are filled. But we could also say, "0.55 of the total seats are filled."
     - Similarly, we can say "0.45 of the seats are unfilled" rather than "45% of the seats are unfilled".
     - (Students will encounter problems later where they are given a decimal number of the whole, such as, 0.3 of 60.)
   - Have student find the percentages equivalent to 0.3 and 0.30. Point out that they are the same. Then have them find the percentage equivalent for 0.03.

$$0.55 = \frac{55}{100} = 55\%$$

0.55 of the seats are filled.
0.45 of the seats are unfilled.

$$0.3 = \frac{3}{10} = \frac{30}{100} = 30\%$$

$$0.30 = \frac{30}{100} = 30\%$$

$$0.03 = \frac{3}{100} = 3\%$$

2. Discuss **tasks 5-6, textbook p. 27**.
   - After students have finished task 6, ask them if they have found a short-cut for writing a decimal as a percentage. They can simply move the decimal point over two places to the right.

3. Discuss expressing a percentage as a decimal number.
   - Write a percentage, such as 4%, on the board.
   - Ask students to write it as a fraction, and then as a decimal.
   - Have them find 40% as a decimal and compare to 4%.

$$4\% = \frac{4}{100} = 0.04$$

$$40\% = \frac{40}{100} = 0.4$$

4. Discuss **tasks 7-8, textbook p. 27**.
   - After students have finished task 8, ask them if they have found a short-cut for writing a percentage as a decimal. They can simply move the decimal point over two places to the left.

Workbook Exercise 16

Activity 2.1c **Percent and fraction**

1. Discuss expressing a percentage as a fraction in its simplest form.
   - Display a 10×10 grid and color in 25 of the squares.
   - Have students find the percentage of the total that is shaded.
   - Have them express this as a fraction out of 100, and then simplify.
   - Have students also find the percentage of the total and fraction of the total that is not shaded.
   - Provide additional examples.

$$25\% = \frac{25}{100} = \frac{1}{4}$$

$\frac{1}{4}$ of the total is shaded

$\frac{3}{4}$ of the total is not shaded

2. Have students do **tasks 9-10, textbook p. 27** and **problems 2-4, Practice 2A, textbook p. 32**.

Workbook Exercise 17

Part 2: Writing Fractions as Percentages — 3 sessions

Objectives

- Express a fraction as a percentage.
- Solve word problems that involve finding the percentage for a part of a whole.

Materials

- 10×10 grids
- Displayable 10x10 grids

Homework

- Workbook Exercise 18
- Workbook Exercise 19
- Workbook Exercise 20

Notes

In this section, students will learn to convert fractions which have a denominator other than 10 or 100 into a percentage. There are 3 methods.

Method 1

Find an equivalent fraction with a denominator of 100 and then write the fraction as a percentage.

$$\frac{1}{4} = \frac{25}{100} = 25\%$$

Method 2

Multiply the fraction by 100%.

$$\frac{1}{4} \times 100\% = 25\%$$

When we speak of percentage, we can think of a whole as divided into 100 parts or units, each with a value of 1%. $\frac{1}{4}$ of this whole is $\frac{1}{4}$ of 100 parts which is 25 parts, or 25%.

Method 3

Divide the fraction to change it to a decimal. Then, write the decimal as a percentage.

$$\frac{1}{4} = 0.25 = 25\%$$

0.25 of the whole is $0.25 \times 100\%$ of the whole. So, we can convert a decimal to a percentage by multiplying it by 100. This is the same as moving the number's decimal point over two places to the right.

The first method can be used when it is easy to find an equivalent fraction with a denominator of 100. The second method is easier to use when it is not as convenient to find the equivalent fraction with a denominator of 100.

When using the second method, students can simplify before multiplying or dividing.

$$\frac{3}{5} \text{ of } 100\% = \frac{3}{\cancel{5}_1} \times \cancel{100}^{20}\% = 60\%$$

The third method, converting the fraction to a decimal first, common in the U.S., is not emphasized in this curriculum. It is similar to the second method, except that there are now two steps, first dividing by a fraction, then multiplying by 100 to get the percentage. The second method, where both steps are combined, offers more opportunities for simplifying the calculations.

Students should be able to easily find the percent of each of the following fractions. Once they know the percent equivalents for $\frac{1}{2}, \frac{1}{4}, \frac{3}{4}$, and $\frac{1}{5}$, they can work the others out from those.

$$\frac{1}{4} = 25\%;\ \frac{1}{2} = \frac{2}{4} = \frac{5}{10} = 50\%;\ \frac{3}{4} = 75\%;\ \frac{1}{5} = \frac{2}{10} = 20\%;\ \frac{2}{5} = \frac{4}{10} = 40\%;$$

$$\frac{3}{5} = \frac{6}{10} = 60\%;\ \frac{4}{5} = \frac{8}{10} = 80\%;\ \frac{1}{10} = 10\%;\ \frac{3}{10} = 30\%;\ \frac{7}{10} = 70\%;\ \frac{9}{10} = 90\%$$

Students will be solving word problems involving percentages. In these word problems, the total is divided up into two or three parts and they are asked to find what percent the unknown parts are. For example, in a collection of 50 red, blue, and green marbles, 10 are red and 25 are blue. They are asked to find what percent of the total are green marbles.

To do this, they can first find the percentage of the total (50) that is red and blue marbles.

Number of red and blue marbles = 10 + 25 = 35

Percentage red and blue marbles = $\frac{35}{50} \times 100\% = 70\%$

Then they subtract the percentage of red and blue marbles from 100% (the total percentage) to find the percent of the total that are green marbles.

Percentage green marbles = 100% - 70% = 30%

Or, they can find the number of green marbles first, and then the percentage.

Number of green marbles = 50 − 10 − 25 = 15

Percentage green marbles = $\frac{15}{50} \times 100\% = 30\%$

When doing word problems which involve finding the percentage for a part of the whole, make sure students know which amount is the whole; that is, what is the total amount that we are finding a percentage of. You may want to call it the *base*. It will be the amount that goes in the denominator of the fraction. At this level, it is always the larger amount, but in *Primary Mathematics 6A* they will be using percentages that are greater than 100%, so the whole may be the smaller number. Therefore, don't have students simply look for the larger number as the whole.

Activity 2.2a **Fractions to percents**

1. Discuss methods to express a fraction as a percentage.
   - Refer to **textbook, p. 28**.
   - Method 1: The fraction is first expressed as an equivalent fraction with denominator of 100. Tell students they can imagine the whole fence as divided into 100 parts. Each fourth is 25 parts, and so $\frac{3}{4}$ is $\frac{75}{100}$. He painted 75% of the fence.

$\frac{3}{4} = \frac{75}{100} = 75\%$

   - Method 2: Tell students to again think of the wall as divided into 100 parts. Since percentage means the number of parts out of 100, each part is 1%, and the total is 100%. To find out how many of these parts there are in $\frac{3}{4}$ of the wall, we find $\frac{3}{4}$ of the total 100 parts, or $\frac{3}{4} \times 100\%$. We can simplify before multiplying

$\frac{3}{4} = \frac{3}{\cancel{4}_1} \times \cancel{100}^{25}\%$
$= (3 \times 25)\%$
$= 75\%$

   - Method 3: You can also show the third method for finding percentage here. Write the division equation for $\frac{3}{4}$ and solve. The answer is 0.75, which is 75%.

$$\begin{array}{r} 0.75 \\ 4\overline{)3.00} \\ \underline{2\ 8} \\ 20 \end{array}$$

$\frac{3}{4} = 0.75 = 75\%$

   - Discuss **tasks 1-2, textbook p. 29**.
   - Task 1 illustrates the first method.
   - Task 2 shows both methods 1 and 2. You can illustrate this task by drawing a 5×5 square grid and shading in 7 squares. Then, divide each square into 4 parts. There are now 100 equal parts. For method 1, we find the equivalent fraction. For method 2, we find the number of 1% parts that are shaded as a fraction of all 100 of them.
   - Ask students to try both methods to find $\frac{24}{40}$ as a percentage. 40 is not a factor of 100.
     - To use the first method, we could first simplify $\frac{24}{40}$ to $\frac{12}{20}$ or $\frac{6}{10}$, and then find the equivalent fraction $\frac{60}{100}$.

$\frac{24}{40} = \frac{6}{10} = \frac{60}{100} = 60\%$
$\frac{24}{40} = \frac{24}{40} \times 100\% = 60\%$

     - For the second method, there are several ways we can simplify $\frac{24}{40} \times 100\%$, such as $\frac{24}{4\cancel{0}} \times 10\cancel{0} = \frac{\cancel{24}^6}{\cancel{4}_1} \times 10 = 6 \times 10 = 60\%$. Using this second method gives us more options for simplifying, since we can use either $\frac{100}{40}$ or $\frac{24}{40}$ first in simplifying.

2. Discuss simple word problems which involve percentage.
   - Discuss **task 3, textbook p. 29**.

- Provide a few other examples. You can use **problems 5, 6,** and **11, Practice 2A, textbook p. 32**.

3. Have students do **task 4, textbook p. 29.**

   Workbook Exercise 18

Activity 2.2b **Fractions to percentage**

1. Discuss expressing a proper fraction with a denominator larger than 100 as a percentage.
   - Discuss **task 5, textbook p. 30**. In this task, the whole is divided into 300 parts. To find the percentage of the colored part, we write it as a fraction.
   - In method 1, we find an equivalent fraction with a denominator of 100. We need to divide both the numerator and denominator by 3.
   - In method 2, we find the fraction of 100%. We can simplify the equation in several ways.
   - You can have students think of this as "merging" 3 units together in order to have 100 units, each of which is 1%.

$$\frac{180}{300}\times 100\% = \frac{180\times 1\cancel{00}}{3\cancel{00}}\% = \frac{180}{3}\% = 60\%$$

$$\frac{18\cancel{0}}{30\cancel{0}}\times 100\% = \frac{18}{30}\times 100\% = \frac{3}{\cancel{5}_1}\times \cancel{100}^{20}\% = (3\times 20)\% = 60\%$$

2. Discuss **task 6, textbook p. 30**.
3. Have students do **task 7, textbook p. 30.**
   - You can have them use both methods to solve each of these, and then explain why they think one or the other method is better for a particular problem.
   - You can have them also do **problem 1, Practice 2A, textbook p. 32**.

   Workbook Exercise 19

Activity 2.2c **Word Problems**

1. Discuss **task 8, textbook p. 31**.
   - Have students also give the fraction of each bar that is shaded, as well as the percentage.
   - Then, have them find the unshaded percentage and fraction of each bar.
   - Encourage students to memorize common fraction/decimal/percent equivalents. It is sometimes easier to solve word problems which involve percentages by converting to fractions.

2. Discuss **tasks 9-11, textbook p. 31**.
   In these problems, emphasize the total, or whole. We are finding the percentage of a specified whole.

3. Have students do **problems 7-13, Practice 2A, textbook p. 32** and share their solutions.

   Workbook Exercise 20

$\frac{1}{4} = 25\%$

$\frac{1}{2} = \frac{5}{10} = 50\%$

$\frac{3}{4} = 75\%$

$\frac{1}{5} = \frac{2}{10} = 20\%$ $\frac{1}{10} = 10\%$

$\frac{2}{5} = \frac{4}{10} = 40\%$ $\frac{3}{10} = 30\%$

$\frac{3}{5} = \frac{6}{10} = 60\%$ $\frac{7}{10} = 70\%$

$\frac{4}{5} = \frac{8}{10} = 80\%$ $\frac{9}{10} = 90\%$

Part 3: Percentage of a Quantity — 4 sessions

Objectives

- Find the value for a percentage part when given the value for the whole.
- Solve word problems involving finding a percentage part of a whole.
- Solve word problems involving tax, interest, discount, increase, decrease.

Materials

- 10×10 grids
- Displayable blank 10x10 grids

Homework

- Workbook Exercise 21
- Workbook Exercise 22
- Workbook Exercise 23
- Workbook Exercise 24

Notes

There are three methods for finding the value of a percentage part of a whole: the fraction method, the unitary method, and the decimal method.

Find the value of 40% of 180.

Fraction method

Convert the percentage to a fraction and then find the fraction of the whole.

$$40\% \text{ of } 180 = \frac{4\cancel{0}}{10\cancel{0}} \times 180 = \frac{4 \times 18\cancel{0}}{1\cancel{0}} = 72$$

Note that we can save a step in simplifying by crossing out equal numbers of 0's in both the numerator and denominator even if one 0 comes from the numerator of the fraction, and the other from the whole number.

$$\frac{40 \times 180}{100} = \frac{4 \times 1\cancel{0} \times 18 \times 1\cancel{0}}{1\cancel{0}\cancel{0}} = 4 \times 18 = 72$$

Unitary method

Find the value of 1% by division, and then multiply to find the value of more than 1%.

$$\begin{aligned} 100\% \text{ of } 180 &= 180 \\ 1\% \text{ of } 180 &= \frac{180}{100} = 1.8 \\ 40\% \text{ of } 180 &= 1.8 \times 40 = 72 \end{aligned}$$

When this method is done in two steps, it often involves multiplying a decimal number by a whole number.

To simplify calculations, the division step and the multiplication step can be combined.

$$40\% \text{ of } 180 = \frac{18\not{0}}{1\not{0}\not{0}} \times 4\not{0} = 72$$

When the percentage we want to find is a multiple of 10, we can first find the value for 10% instead of 1%.

$$100\% \longrightarrow 180$$
$$10\% \longrightarrow 18$$
$$40\% \longrightarrow 18 \times 4 = 72$$

However, always finding 1% first has a conceptual advantage; it keeps students aware of the underlying information. They do not get confused by the process into just pushing numbers around.

Decimal method

Convert the percentage to a decimal and multiply the decimal by the whole.

$$40\% \text{ of } 180 = 0.40 \times 180 = 72$$

In this curriculum, the decimal method isn't used at this level. Instead, the fraction method will be used primarily. The unitary method will become more important in *Primary Mathematics 6*. Allow students to use either the fraction method or the unitary method.

The fractions in these exercises and later ones can be solved in more than one way. For example,

$$\frac{15}{10\not{0}} \times 4\not{0} = \frac{15 \times \not{4}^{2}}{\not{10}_{5}} = \frac{\not{15}^{3} \times 2}{\not{5}_{1}} = 6$$

$$\frac{\not{15}^{3}}{\not{100}_{20}} \times 40 = \frac{3 \times \not{40}^{2}}{\not{20}_{1}} = 6$$

Simplifying the fraction as much as possible before performing other operations will make the multiplication easier.

Students will learn to solve problems involving tax, interest, discount, increase, and decrease. Students will become familiar with these terms through sufficient discussion.

Activity 2.3a **Percentage part**

1. Use **p. 33 in the textbook** to discuss two methods for finding the percentage of a quantity.

Method 1:

- Ask students what the total is. It is 500. Tell students that if we divide the total by 100, we will get the number of people in 1%. One way to look at this is to say that the bar representing 500 has 100 equal units. There are 100 units, and each unit is 1%. To find the value of 1 unit, we divide the total by the number of units. So to find the value of 1%, we divide the total, 500, by 100.

$$100\% \text{ of } 500 = 100 \text{ units} = 500$$
$$1\% \text{ of } 500 = 1 \text{ unit} = \frac{500}{100} = 5$$

- Once we know the value of 1 unit, or 1%, (5 people) we can find the value of 30 units, or 30%, by multiplying the value for 1 unit by 30.

$$30\% \text{ of } 500 = 30 \text{ units} = 5 \times 30 = 150$$

There were 150 children.

- For this particular problem, we could first find the value of 10 units by dividing 500 by 10, then the value of 3 of those 10 units to get 30%.

$$100\% \text{ of } 500 = 100 \text{ units} = 500$$
$$10\% \text{ of } 500 = 10 \text{ units} = \frac{500}{10} = 50$$
$$30\% \text{ of } 500 = 30 \text{ units} = 50 \times 3 = 150$$

Method 2:

- Since percentage is one way of representing a fraction with a denominator of 100, we can find 30% of 500 by finding $\frac{30}{100}$ of 500.
- We can still think of the total as being divided into 100 equal units. We want to find the value of 30 out of 100 of them.
- Discuss steps for finding $\frac{30}{100} \times 500$. Students should simplify first. There are several ways to simplify the expression.

$$30\% \text{ of } 500 = \frac{30}{100} \times 500 = \frac{30}{1\cancel{00}} \times 5\cancel{00} = 30 \times 5 = 150$$

2. Discuss **task 1, textbook p. 34.** Have students use both methods to solve the problem.

Method 1:

- Find 1% of 120, and then 90% of 120.

$$100\% \text{ of } 120 = 120$$
$$1\% \text{ of } 120 = \frac{120}{100} = 1.2$$
$$90\% \text{ of } 120 = 1.2 \times 90 = 108$$

- Point out that in the first method we do not have to solve the division right away; we can write it as a fraction and simplify later.

$$1\% \text{ of } 120 = \frac{120}{100}$$
$$90\% \text{ of } 120 = \frac{12\cancel{0}}{1\cancel{0}\cancel{0}} \times 9\cancel{0} = 12 \times 9 = 108$$

Method 2:

- Find $\frac{90}{100}$ of 120.

90% of $120 = \frac{90}{100} \times 120 = 108$

- Point out that the difference between the two methods is simply whether we show 120 divided by 100 and then multiplied by 90, or 90 divided by 100 and then multiplied by 120. Both methods give the same answer, and both expressions could be simplified the same way.

$\frac{120}{100} \times 90 = \frac{90}{100} \times 120 = \frac{90 \times 120}{100}$

- Ask students how many failed the physical fitness test (10%). Point out that an easy way to solve this problem is to find the number that failed, as 10% of 120, and subtract that from the total.

10% of $120 = 12$
$120 - 12 = 108$

3. Discuss **task 2, textbook p. 34.** Have students use both methods to solve the problem.

4. Have students do **task 3, textbook p. 34.**
   - Encourage students to use mental math when possible.
     - Students should realize that to find 1% of a number, they can simply move the decimal point two places to the left. Or, if the number is in hundreds, take off two zeros.
     - To find 10% of a number, they can move the decimal point over one place to the left, or they can take off a 0 in the ones place. For example, in 3.(a), 10% of 300 is 30; and 5% is half of that, or 15.
     - They can also solve these problems by using the equivalent fraction. For example, in 3.(d), 25% is equivalent to $\frac{1}{4}$, so they can simply divide 40 m by 4. In 2.(f), 75% is equivalent to $\frac{3}{4}$, so they can divide 400 g by 4, which is 100 g, then multiply by 3, to get 300 g.
   - You can also have students do **problem 1, Practice 2B, textbook p. 37**.

Workbook Exercise 21

Activity 2.3b **Word problems**

1. Discuss **tasks 4-5, textbook pp. 34-35.**
   - For task 5, two methods are given. In the first one, we first find the percent of the members that are adults, and then use that percentage to find the number of adults. In the second method, we first use the percentage of children to find the number of children, and then we find the number of adults.
   - Provide additional examples. You can use **problems 2-7, Practice 2B, textbook p. 37**.

Workbook Exercise 22

Activity 2.3c **Tax and discounts**

1. Discuss the concept of interest rate. Not many of the students will have had any experience with interest rates, so you will need to explain the concept to them.
   - Interest rates are the percentage *earned* (in one year) on the amount of money invested. At the same time, interest rates are the percentage *paid* (in one year) on the amount borrowed, by the borrower. So at the end of one year, the borrower will owe the lender the original amount borrowed, plus the interest. This original amount is the base, or the whole. Emphasize the amount that is the whole, or 100%, in all of these problems. Determining the total, or base, in a percentage problem will become more important in *Primary Mathematics 6* where the base might change within a problem.
   - Provide a problem that is easy to calculate mentally. For example:
     - Tell students that the interest rate on $100 is 10% a year. This means that if the account holder puts $100 in the bank and leaves it there all year, the bank will pay him 10% of that amount for having it in their bank. The money he initially puts in is an investment; the interest is the money he earns on that investment. So at the end of one year, he will have a total of the money he first put into the bank, plus the interest.
     - Ask students to find 10% of $100

       Interest = 10% of $100
= $10
     - This is the amount that the bank pays the account holder for putting $100 in its bank for one year. The account holder will earn $10. The payment is made by adding it to the original amount in the bank.
     - Ask students how much money the account holder will have in the account at the end of the year, after the interest is paid.

       Total amount = $100 + $10
= $110
   - It is better that the students understand the concept than simply having a formula to plug numbers into, such as "Total = investment + interest".
   - Provide a few other examples that are easy to compute, such as 5% interest on $200.
2. Discuss **task 6, textbook p. 35**.
3. Discuss the concept of discount.
   - Students may not have had much experience with discounts. Discuss "sales" and when they are likely to occur, such as 10% off for winter clothes at the end of the season.
   - Provide a problem involving discounts that is easy to calculate, for example:
   - Tell students that you got a 10% discount on $100 worth of clothing. The whole that we will take a percentage of is the initial cost of the clothing.
     - Ask them to find 10% of $100.
     - This amount is called the discount. It is how much is "taken off" of the cost.

       Discount = 10% of $100
= $10
     - Ask students to find the final cost. The result is the amount spent on the clothing.

       Final cost = $100 - $10
= $90
   - Provide a few more simple problems so that students can focus on the concept rather than the computation.
4. Discuss **task 7, textbook p. 36**.
5. Have students do **problems 9-10, Practice 2B, textbook p. 37**.

Workbook Exercise 23

Activity 2.3d **Increase and decrease**

1. Discuss the concept of percent increase.
   - Discuss situations in which an amount might increase by a certain percentage. For example, a person's salary could go up 5%, or rent, or the overall cost of living.
   - Provide a simple problem involving percent increase, for example:
   - Tell students that a family pays $400 a month on health insurance, and just found out that its cost would increase by 15%. How much will the family now have to pay?
     - Ask them to find 15% of $400.
     - You might want to point out that one mental math approach to the calculations is to find 10%, which is $40, and add half of $40 (5%) to get $60.
     - This amount is called the increase. It is the amount that will be added to the initial amount.
     - Ask students to find the final amount. The result is the new cost of health insurance.

     Cost now = $400
     Increase = 15% of $400
     = $60

     New cost = $400 + $60
     = $460
   - Provide a few more examples that are easy to calculate.

2. Discuss **task 8, textbook p. 36**.

3. Discuss percent decrease.
   - Discuss situations in which an amount might decrease by a certain percentage. For example, enrollment in a school might go down by 5%.
   - Discuss **task 9, textbook p. 36**.
   - 400 is the whole. The decrease is a percentage of the whole. The final amount is the initial amount minus the decrease.
   - Discuss the following situation.
     - We start with 100 and decrease that by 10%.
     - Then we increase this new amount by 10%.
     - Will we have what we start with?
     - No, because the new amount after the decrease was 90, but an increase of 10% of 90 is 9, so we end up with 99, not the original 100.
     - It is important to know what it is we are decreasing or increasing; that is, what number we are finding a percentage of, or what our whole is.
     - The original whole that we decreased was 100, but the new whole that we increased was only 90.
     - So a decrease followed by an increase by the same percent does not give the original amount. Similarly, an increase followed by a decrease by the same percent will not give the original amount.

4. Have students do **problems 11-13, Practice 2B, textbook p. 37**, and any other problems in this practice not yet completed. Have students share their methods.

Workbook Exercise 24

Unit 3 – Average

Objectives

- Find the average of a set of data.
- Find the average when given the total and the number of items.
- Find the total when given the average and the number of items.
- Solve problems that involve averages and measurement in compound units.
- Solve word problems of up to 3-steps that involve averages.

Suggested number of sessions: 6

	Objectives	Textbook	Workbook	Activities
Part 1 : Average				**6 sessions**
29	▪ Understand average.	p. 38 pp. 38-40, tasks 1-3	Ex. 25	3.1a
30	▪ Find the average of a set of data.	p. 40, tasks 4-5	Ex. 26	3.1b
31	▪ Find the average when given the total and the number of items. ▪ Find the total when given the average and the number of items.	pp. 40-41, tasks 6-8 p. 43, Practice 3A, 1-4	Ex. 27	3.1c
32	▪ Multiply and divide in compound units. ▪ Solve problems that involve averages and compound units of measurement.	pp. 41-42, tasks 9-12 p. 43, Practice 3A, 5-6	Ex. 28	3.1d
33	▪ Find the average of a set of data that involve measurements in compound units		Ex. 29	3.1e
34	▪ Solve word problems that involve averages.	p. 42, tasks 13-14 p. 43, Practice 3A, 7-8	Ex. 30	3.1f

Part 1: Average — 6 sessions

Objectives

- Understand the concept of average.
- Find the average of a set of data.
- Find the average when given the total and the number of items.
- Find the total when given the average and the number of items.
- Solve problems that involve averages and measurement in compound units.
- Solve word problems of up to 3-steps that involve averages.

Materials

- Counters that can be displayed
- Paper bowls or plates
- Measuring tools – yard stick, meter stick, stopwatch, etc.

Homework

- Workbook Exercise 25
- Workbook Exercise 26
- Workbook Exercise 27
- Workbook Exercise 28
- Workbook Exercise 29
- Workbook Exercise 30

Notes

Average is the arithmetical mean of a set of data.

We can think of a "set of data" as any list consisting of individual or grouped items. Anything can be used as a set of data. Data can be information about individuals, such as the weight or height of each student in a classroom. Data can be information about groups, such as the number of bicycles owned by children in different classrooms, or the number of stores their families shop in, or the number of rainy days in different months.

To find the average for a set of data, we first find the sum of the individual items on the list, and then divide that sum by the number of items on the list.

$$\text{Average} = \text{Total of items} \div \text{Number of items}$$

For example: If 4 boys' ages were 10, 13, 11, and 9, their average age is found by first adding the 4 ages together and then dividing by 4.

$$(10 + 13 + 11 + 9) \div 4 = 43 \div 4 = 10.75 \text{ years}$$

This equation can be written as $\frac{10+13+11+9}{4} = \frac{43}{4} = 10.75$

The boys' average age is 10.75, while their actual ages vary. Note that an average does not have to be a whole number, even though the list's items may all be whole numbers.

If, instead, we are given the set of data's average, and the number of items in the set of data, we can find the total by multiplying the average by the number of items.

Total of items = Average $\times$ number of items

For example: If the average age of 4 boys is 10.75, we can find the sum of their ages by multiplying the average age by the number of boys:

Total = $10.75 \times 4 = 43$

Students learned to multiply and divide in compound units in *Primary Mathematics 4*. This is reviewed here in the context of averages.

To *multiply* compound units, we multiply the different units separately, and then carry out any necessary conversions.

For example: If the average weight of 3 packages is 1 kg 400 g, we find the total weight by multiplying 1 kg 400 g by 3.

Multiply the kg: 1 kg $\times$ 3 = 3 kg
Multiply the g: 400 g $\times$ 3 = 1200 g
Convert to compound units: 1200 g = 1 kg 200 g
Add together: 3 kg + 1 kg 200 g = 4 kg 200 g
So 1 kg 400 g $\times$ 3 = 4 kg 200 g

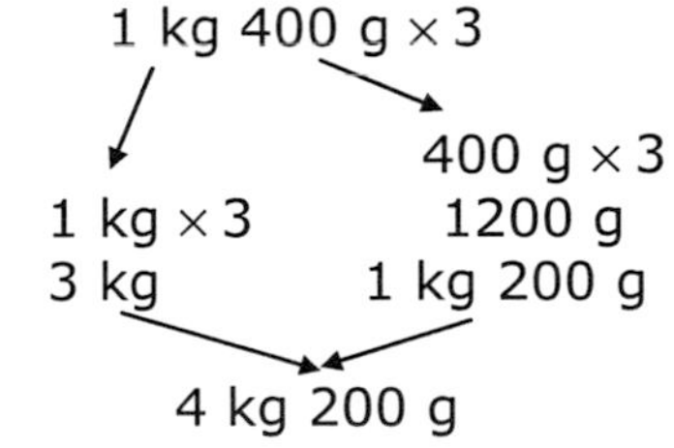

To *divide* compound units, first we divide the larger unit; then we convert any remainder into the smaller unit and add the smaller units together; then we divide these smaller units.

For example: If the total weight of 4 packages is 5 kg 200g, to find the average weight of the packages we need to divide 5 kg 200 g by 4.

Divide the kg first:
5 kg ÷ 4 = 1 kg remainder 1 kg
Change the remainder into g and add to the 200 g:
1000 g + 200 g = 1200 g
Divide the grams:
1200 g ÷ 4 = 300 g
Add together: 1 kg + 300 g
So 5 kg 200 g ÷ 4 = 1 kg 300 g

5 kg 200 g ÷ 4
5 kg ÷ 4
1 kg 1000 g 200 g
1200 g ÷ 4
300 g
1 kg 300 g

As you do this section, you can have students record the high and low temperatures for each day. At the end of this unit, they can compute the average high and low temperatures for the period. Save the data and use it in unit 5 to construct line graphs.

Activity 3.1a **Average**

1. Illustrate the concept of average with concrete examples.
   - Use counters which you can group within circles, or linking cubes that you can put together to show various lengths. The discussion which follows assumes counters placed in circles. Students can work in groups or pairs
   - Have students draw 5 circles on paper, or provide each group with 5 paper plates (or bowls) to use as circles. Have them put 2 objects in one circle, 3 in the next, 4 in the next, 5 in the next, and 6 in the last circle.
   - Ask students for the total number of counters.

     $2 + 3 + 4 + 5 + 6 = 20$
     The **sum** of 2, 3, 4, 5, and 6 is 20.
   - Then ask students to rearrange the counters so that each circle has the same number of counters.
   - Tell students that the number of counters now in each circle is the number that would be in each circle if the total number, 20, were divided evenly among the 5 circles.

     $\frac{2+3+4+5+6}{5} = 4$
     The **average** of 2, 3, 4, 5, and 6 is 4.
   - This number is called the *average* of the original numbers.
   - Draw a bar on the board and divide it up into 5 parts of varying sizes: 2, 3, 4, 5, and 6. Then, draw another bar below it and divide it up into 5 equal units. Tell student that when we find the average, we are evening out the amount in each part of the first bar.

2	3	4	5	6
4	4	4	4	4

   - When each number is replaced by the average number, the sum of the numbers remains unchanged.

     $2 + 3 + 4 + 5 + 6 = 20$
     $4 + 4 + 4 + 4 + 4 = 20$
   - Write a set of numbers, such as 4, 6, and 11, on the board and have students use their counters to find the average, and then see that finding the answer by calculation gives the same answer.
   - Provide additional examples. If students have plenty of concrete experience, they will be able to find some simple averages mentally. For example, if they need to find the average of 8, 10, and 12, they could mentally "see" that it would be 10 right away by taking 2 "off" of from the 12 and putting it "on" the 8. Or, they can find the average of 4, 7, and 7 by mentally taking 1 off from each of the 7's and putting it onto the 4.

2. Discuss **textbook p. 38** and **tasks 1-3, textbook pp. 39-40**.

Workbook Exercise 25

Activity 3.1b **Average of data**

1. Find the average of a set of data.
   Have students collect a set of data and then find its average.
   - For example, you can ask four students for the number of books they read last week, or the number of rooms in their homes, or the number of minutes each takes to get from home to school.
   - You can use data that involve measurement, but for now do not use compound units. For example, you can have the students work in groups and measure how far each student can step, or the length of each student's forearm, in centimeters or inches only (not in meters and centimeters, or feet and inches).
   - As students find the average of the data the class collects, point out that an average is not always a whole number, even if the data values are all whole numbers. Have students round the averages to two decimal places.
   - Have students determine if their averages make sense. Bring up the following points:
     - The average should not be higher than the highest number or lower than the lowest number.
     - If more of the data values are at the higher end of the range of values, the average will be higher also.
     - An "outlying" value can draw the average down or up. For example, if the numbers of trees in 4 students' yards are 0, 8, 10, and 12, the average is 7.5. This is less than 3 out of the 4 values, because the far-out value 0 pulls the average down.
     - Just because the average number of trees is 7.5, that does not mean that there are half-trees. We may hear that the average number of children per couple in some country is 2.3, but we know there isn't a single three tenths of a child running around, anywhere.

2. Discuss **tasks 4-5, textbook p. 40**.

   Workbook Exercise 26

Activity 3.1c **Find the total from the average**

1. Discuss finding the total when given the average and the number of data points.
   - Draw 5 circles on the board and tell students that you have counters in each circle, but don't know how many. There could be 9 in one, 5 in another, and so on. You do know that the average number of counters in each circle is 10.
   - Ask how you can find the total number of counters. Multiply the average (10) by the number of circles (5). The total number of counters is 50.
   - Point out that we are able to find the total number of counters even if we don't know how many there are in the different circles if we are given the average.
   - Repeat with another example. Tell them that 20 books are piled on top of each other. The average thickness of each book is 3 cm. How high is the pile of books? (60 cm). (US: The average thickness per book is 1.5 in. The pile is 30 inches high, or 2 ft. 6 in.)

2. Discuss **tasks 6-8, textbook pp. 40-41**.

3. Have students do **problem 1-4, Practice 3A, textbook p. 43**.

   Workbook Exercise 27

Activity 3.1d **Multiply and divide in compound units**

1. Discuss **tasks 9-12, textbook pp. 41-42**.
   - Make sure students understand the steps involved in multiplying or dividing in compound units.
   - Task 9:
     - Number of items = 3.
     - Average weight = 1 kg 400 g.
     - Multiply the kg: 1 kg × 3 = 3 kg
     - Multiply the g: 400 g × 3 = 1200 g
     - Convert to compound units: 1200 g = 1 kg 200 g
     - Add together: 3 kg + 1 kg 200 g = 4 kg 200 g
     - So the total weight is 4 kg 200 g

1 kg 400 g × 3
1 kg × 3
3 kg
400 g × 3
1200 g
1 kg 200 g
4 kg 200 g

   - Task 10:
     - Number of items = 4
     - Total weight = 5 kg 200 g.
     - Divide the kg first: 5 kg ÷ 4 = 1 kg remainder 1 kg
     - Convert the remainder to g and add to the 200 g: 1000 g + 200 g = 1200 g
     - Divide the grams: 1200 g ÷ 4 = 300 g
     - Add together: 1 kg + 300 g
     - So their average weight is 1 kg 300 g

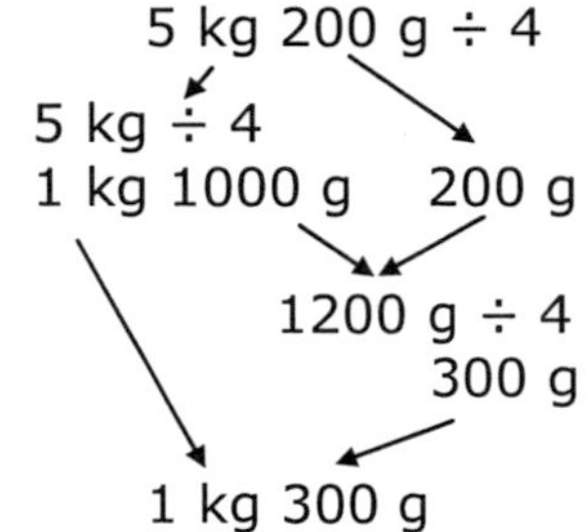

   - Task 11:
     - Distance = 2 km
     - Total cycling time = 15 min 20 s
     - Average time per km is 15 min 20 s ÷ 2
     - Divide minutes: 15 min ÷ 2 = 7 min R 60 s
     - Add seconds together: 60 s + 20 s = 80 s
     - Divide seconds: 80 s ÷ 2 = 40 s
     - Add together: 7 min + 40 s = 7 min 40 s
     - So the average time per km is 7 min 40 s

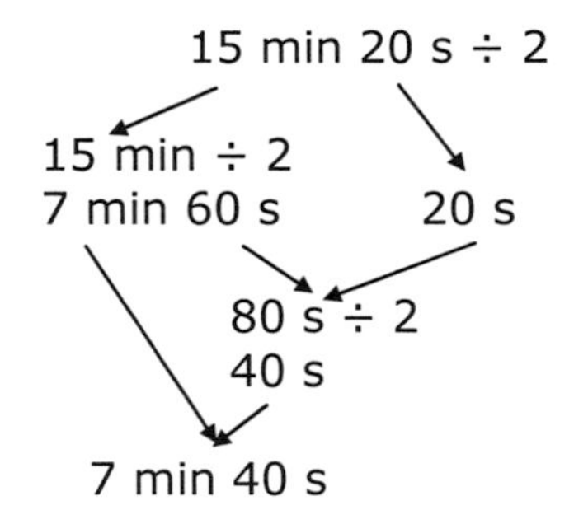

   - Task 12:
     - Distance = 3 km
     - Average cycling time per km = 2 min 45 s
     - Total cycling time is 2 min 45 s × 3
     - Multiply minutes: 2 min × 3 = 6 min
     - Multiply seconds: 45 s × 3 = 135 s
     - Convert: 135 s = 2 min 15 s
     - Add together: 6 min + 2 min 15 s = 8 min 15 s
     - So the total cycling time is 8 min 15 s

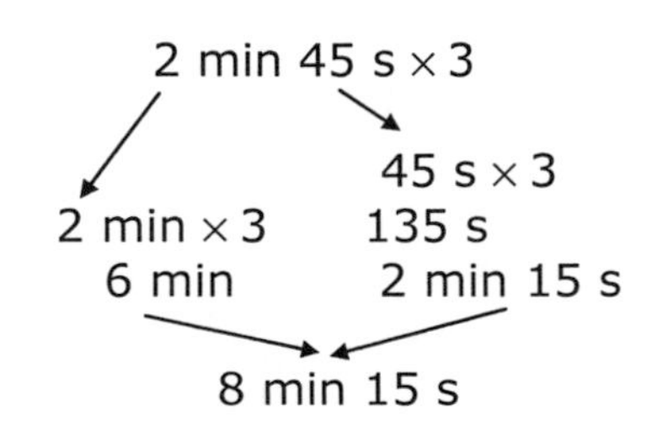

2. Have students do **problems 5-6, Practice 3A, textbook p. 43** and share their solutions.

Workbook Exercise 28

Activity 3.1e **Average of measurement in compound units**

1. Collect data in compound units and find the average.
   - Have students collect a set of data that involves compound units. For example, they can work in groups and measure the height of each person in meters and centimeters or in feet and inches. You may want to do this first as a class activity, using the heights of 3 or 4 students, so you can go over the calculations together with the students.
   - Ask students to find the total for their data, and the average. Have them share their results, including their calculations.
   - Again, have them explain why the average value makes sense based on the data used.

2. Repeat with other data, using a different type of measurement.

Workbook Exercise 29

Activity 3.1f **Word problems**

1. Discuss **tasks 13-14, textbook p. 42.**
   - You can draw circles to help students visualize the problems. Each circle represents or contains differing data values. Mark the average and the totals.

Task 13:

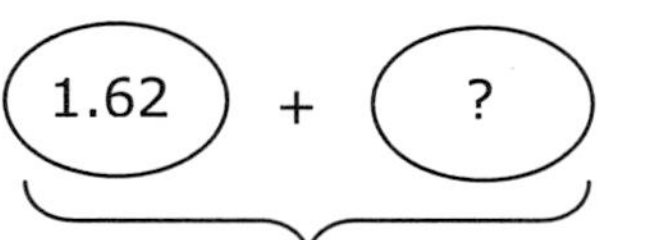

Average height of 2 boys = 1.55 m
Total height = 1.55 m × 2 = 3.10 m

Height of other boy = 3.10 m – 1.62 m = 1.48

   - Point out that, in task 14, we do not have to find the individual prices for the first two books in order to find the answer.

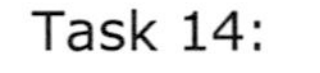

Average cost of 2 books = \$3.90
Total cost of 2 books = \$3.90 × 2 = \$7.80

Average cost of 3 books = \$4.50
Total cost of 3 books = \$4.50 × 3 = \$13.50

Cost of third book = total cost – cost of 2 books
= \$13.50 - \$7.80
= \$5.70

2. Have students do **problems 7-8, Practice 3A**, **textbook p. 43**, and share their solutions.

Workbook Exercise 30

Unit 4 – Rate

Objectives

- Understand rate as one quantity per unit of another quantity.
- Solve word problems that involve rate.

Suggested number of sessions: 6

	Objectives	Textbook	Workbook	Activities
Part 1 : Rate				**6 sessions**
35	▪ Understand rate as one quantity per unit of another quantity.	p. 44 p. 45, tasks 1-2	Ex. 31	4.1a
36	▪ Find a total quantity when given the rate relationship of the different units. ▪ Draw line diagrams for rate problems.	p. 45, tasks 3-4	Ex. 32	4.1b
37	▪ Use an arrow to show the relationship between two quantities in a rate problem. ▪ Solve word problems involving a given rate.	p. 46, tasks 5-6	Ex. 33	4.1c
38	▪ Solve word problem of up to 3-steps that involve rate.	p. 47, tasks 7-8 p. 50, Practice 4A, 1-6	Ex. 34	4.1d
39	▪ Solve problems using rate tables.	pp. 48-49, tasks 9-12 p. 50, Practice 4A, 7-8	Ex. 35	4.1e
40	▪ Practice			4.1f

Part 1: Rate — 6 sessions

Objectives

- Understand rate.
- Find the rate for two linked quantities.
- Solve problems involving rate.

Materials

- Stopwatch
- Rate charts, such as postage rates
- Postage scale (optional)

Homework

- Workbook Exercise 31
- Workbook Exercise 32
- Workbook Exercise 33
- Workbook Exercise 34
- Workbook Exercise 35

Notes

A rate involves two quantities that correspond to each other. It is usually expressed as one quantity (or measurement) per unit of another quantity (or measurement).

Given two quantities A and B such that 5 units of A corresponds to 1 unit of B, we say that the rate is 5 units of A per unit of B. The word "per" means "for every" and can also be written with a "/".

Speed is an example of rate. If a car goes 100 kilometers in 1 hour, the rate is 100 kilometers per hour. The cost of something by weight is another example of rate. If meat costs $6 for each kilogram, we can say that the rate is $6 per kilogram. How fast a person types is another example of rate.

$$50 \text{ words per minute} = 50 \text{ words/min} = 50\,\frac{\text{words}}{\text{min}}$$

We can use an arrow to show the relationship between the two quantities.

50 words $\longrightarrow$ 1 minute

or 1 minute $\longrightarrow$ 50 words

The arrow symbolizes the words "corresponds to" or "per".

For whole-number, fraction, and ratio problems students learned to set up bar models to diagram the pertinent information in these kinds of word problem. Here, students will learn how to use a line model to diagram the information in word problems that involve rate. Drawing a line diagram helps students understand and set up the problem correctly, and, after doing the computations, see at a glance whether their answer is reasonable. The activities in this section contain suggestions for relating line diagrams to the familiar bar models, and finding the rate for a unit quantity to finding the value of one unit in a bar model.

A line model is similar to a number line that has two scales, simultaneously marking two different but linked units.
Example 1:
Paul can type 200 words in 5 minutes. How many words can he type in 3 minutes?

A number line with both types of quantities might look like this:

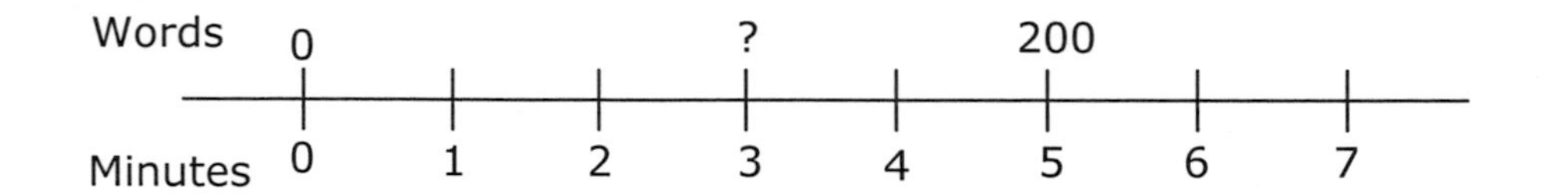

The markings are labeled for minutes on one side of the line and for words on the other side. Since 200 words are typed in 5 minutes, the mark for 200 words is also the one for 5 minutes. The question mark for the number of words typed in 3 minutes is at the same mark as the 3-minute mark. When we know the scale for the top part of the number line, we can find the value at the point indicated by the question mark. In this problem, we can find the scale by dividing 200 by 5, which gives us the number of words that can be typed in 1 minute (40). From there, we find the number of words typed in 3 minutes by multiplying that by 3 ($40 \times 3 = 120$).

In a line diagram, only two marks are used, one for the two known quantities linked in the problems (here, 200 words and 5 minutes) and one for the quantity that needs to be found (indicated with "?") and its linked quantity (here, 3 min). Usually, we put the smaller quantities (3 min. and ? words) at the left mark, and the larger quantities (5 min and 200 words) at the right mark.

? words 200 words

3 min 5 min

Using a line model helps the student write an equation[1]. In Primary Mathematics, a unitary approach is used in solving many word problems. In bar models, if unit bars are used, then the student knows or finds the value for 1 unit. This underlying approach is used for solving rate problems. So here, we find the number of words for 1 minute by dividing 200 (words) by 5 (minutes). This is our unit: 40 words typed in 1 minute. Once we find the value for 1 unit, we can find the value for any number of minutes using multiplication. So 40 x 3 = 120 is the number of words in 3 minutes. We can now replace the question mark with 120.

Students will learn how to show the rate computation with arrows, as follows:

We will put minutes on the left side of the arrow, since we want to find the number of words he types in 1 minute. This is the "unitary" approach to solving rate problems.

$$5 \text{ min} \longrightarrow 200 \text{ words}$$

In one minute he would type a fifth as many words, so we divide by 5. Notice that we carrying out the same operation on the values on both sides of the arrow — we divide the number of minutes by 5 and the number of words by 5.

$$1 \text{ min} \longrightarrow \frac{200}{5} \text{ words}$$

---

[1] In some textbooks, the equation for this problem would be written as a proportion: $\frac{?}{3} = \frac{200}{5}$

Then, we find the value for the number of words typed in 3 minutes. He would type 3 times as many words in 3 minutes as in 1 minute, so we multiply by 3. Again, we are carrying out the same operation on the values on both sides of the arrow.

$$3 \text{ min} \longrightarrow \frac{200}{5} \times 3 \text{ words}$$
$$= 120 \text{ words}$$

He can type 120 words in 3 minutes.

When this process is well understood, the steps in the arrow diagram can be combined.

$$5 \text{ min} \longrightarrow 200 \text{ words}$$
$$3 \text{ min} \longrightarrow \frac{200}{5} \times 3 \text{ words}$$

Example 2:
Paul can type 200 words in 5 minutes. How long will it take him to type 300 words?

From the line diagram, we can see that we need to find the time for typing 300 words, when we know how long it takes him to type 200 words.

200 words — 300 words
5 min — ? min

For this new problem, the rate is minutes per word. We will find the time it takes to type 1 word, and then we will find the time it takes to type 300 words.

Since we want to find the time for typing 1 word, we will put the number of words on the left side of the arrow, and the time on the right side of the arrow.

$$200 \text{ words} \longrightarrow 5 \text{ minutes}$$

If 200 words can be typed in 5 minutes, we can divide 5 by 200 to get the time for 1 word.

$$1 \text{ word} \longrightarrow \frac{5}{200} \text{ min}$$

Then, we find the number of minutes it takes to type 300 words.

$$300 \text{ words} \rightarrow \frac{5}{2\cancel{00}} \times 3\cancel{00} \text{ min}$$
$$= 7.5 \text{ min}$$

Again, we are carrying out the same operation on the values on both sides of the arrow — changing them the same way (dividing by 200, then multiplying by 300) to maintain the relationship.

He will take 7.5 minutes to type 300 words.

Looking back at the line diagram, we see that 7.5 min makes sense, since it is larger than 5 minutes (in the same way that 300 words is larger than 200 words).

Note that we can choose not to solve the intermediate step $\left(\frac{5}{200}\right)$ immediately and instead reduce the fractions at the end, making the calculations simpler.

In teaching students to use line diagrams and arrows to show rate relationships, start with simple problems (that they could probably solve mentally). That way, they can concentrate on learning the new methods first. Once they know the methods, and that they work, they will be comfortable applying them to more complicated problems.

In this unit, students will also have problems involving rate tables. With rate tables, the rate increases in steps, rather then continuously. For example, if the parking costs $1 for each hour, the parking fee for 1 h 20 min is the same as the fee for 2 hours.

Activity 4.1a **Rate**

1. Introduce the concept of rate.
    - Write the problem shown here on the board.

> Mr. Lee bought 60 pens to give equally to his 5 children. How many pens did each child get?

- Let students tell you how to draw the bar model to solve this problem. Write the equations as shown here.

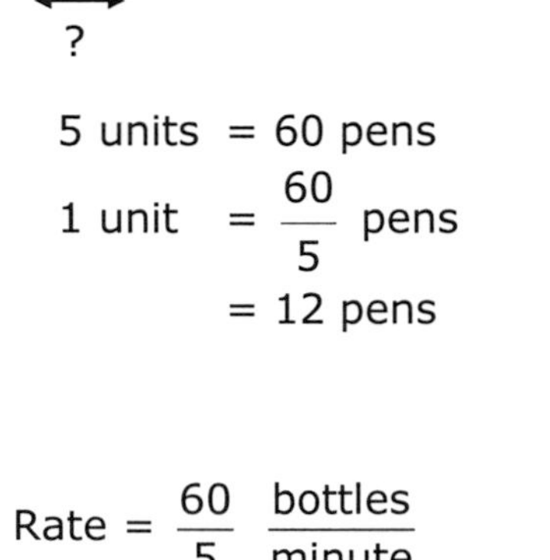

$$\begin{aligned} 5 \text{ units} &= 60 \text{ pens} \\ 1 \text{ unit} &= \frac{60}{5} \text{ pens} \\ &= 12 \text{ pens} \end{aligned}$$

- Discuss the material on **p. 44 of the textbook**. Point out that this example is similar to the one on the board, but instead of finding the number of pens for each child, we are relating the bottles filled to the number of minutes.
    - To find out how many bottles are filled in one minute, we divide the number of bottles filled (60) by the number of minutes it takes (5).
- Tell students that the answer is the **rate** for the number of bottles filled each minute.
- **Rate** is the relationship between two quantities with different measurement units. In this problem, the two units are bottles and minutes.
- We use the word "per" for rate. We say that the rate at which the machine fills the bottles is 12 bottles per minute. Sometimes "per" is written as "/". We can write that the rate is 12 bottles/minute (read as "12 bottles per minute").

$$\begin{aligned} \text{Rate} &= \frac{60}{5}\ \frac{\text{bottles}}{\text{minute}} \\ &= \frac{12}{1}\ \frac{\text{bottles}}{\text{minute}} \\ &= 12 \text{ bottles every 1 minute} \\ &= 12 \text{ bottles per minute} \\ &= 12 \text{ bottles/minute} \end{aligned}$$

- Draw a bar model to illustrate rate.
    - Tell students that since we want to find the number of bottles filled in 1 minute, we could use a unit bar for 1 minute. We need 5 unit bars for 5 minutes. The value of the whole (5 units) is 60 bottles. So, the value of 1 unit bar is $\frac{60}{5}$, or 12 bottles.

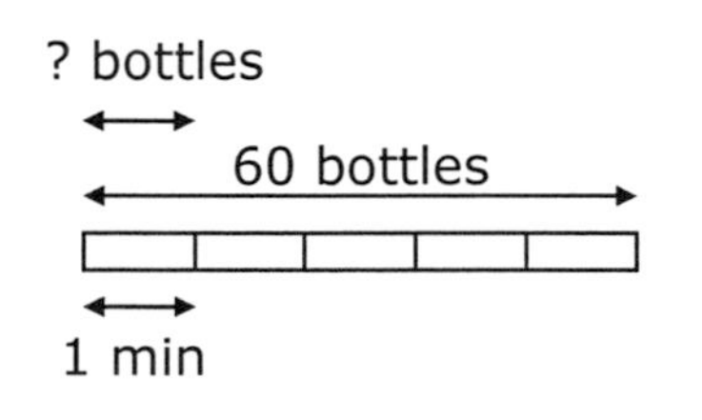

- Discuss other instances where rate is used, such as how fast a person can type in words per minute. Other speeds are an example of rate, such as how fast a car goes in kilometers per hour or miles per hour (speed will be covered in detail in *Primary Mathematics 6*).
- Remind students that in the last unit, they did problems involving interest and tax rates. For example, the interest rate could be 5% per year. In interest and tax rates, one quantity is the percentage of the money invested or earned, and the other is time, often 1 year.

2. Discuss **task 1, textbook p. 45.**
   - We want to find the rate of pay, which is the number of dollars for 1 hour of work. So we find the quotient of dollars divided by hours.

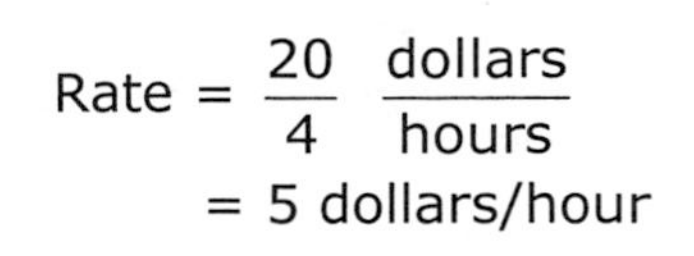

   - Draw a bar diagram to illustrate this problem.

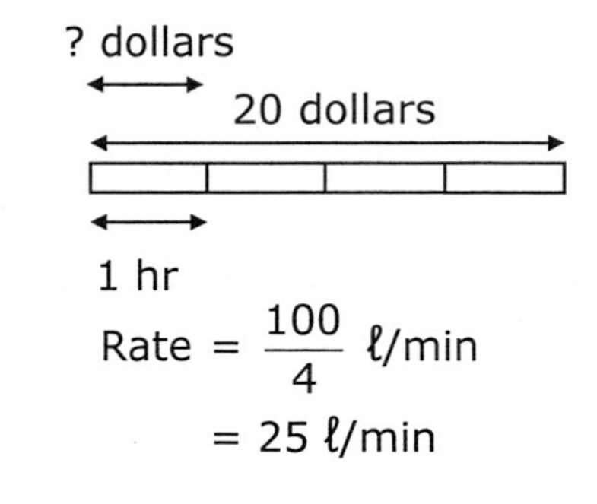

3. Discuss **task 2, textbook p. 45.**
   - Have students draw a model and find the rate.

$$\text{Rate} = \frac{100}{4}\ \ell/\text{min}$$
$$= 25\ \ell/\text{min}$$

4. If there is time, have students do Workbook Exercise 31, parts (a) and (b) and share their solutions. Otherwise, assign this as homework.

Workbook Exercise 31

Activity 4.1b **Rate problems**

1. Discuss **task 3, textbook p. 45** and introduce line diagrams.
   - In this task, we are given the rate (120 cars per minute) and asked to find how many cars the machine makes in 6 minutes.
   - Show students that a diagram will help us see what equation we should use.
     - We can diagram this by making 1 unit represent the number of toy cars made in 1 minute, i.e. 1 unit = 120 cars.
     - The number of toy cars made in 6 minutes is 6×120, or 720 cars.

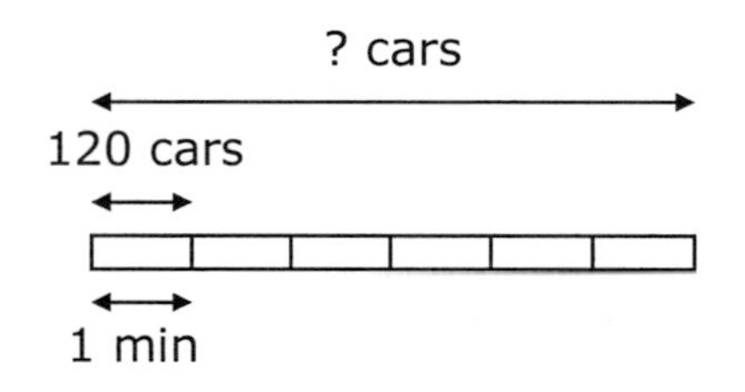

   - Write the two equations shown here at the right on the board.

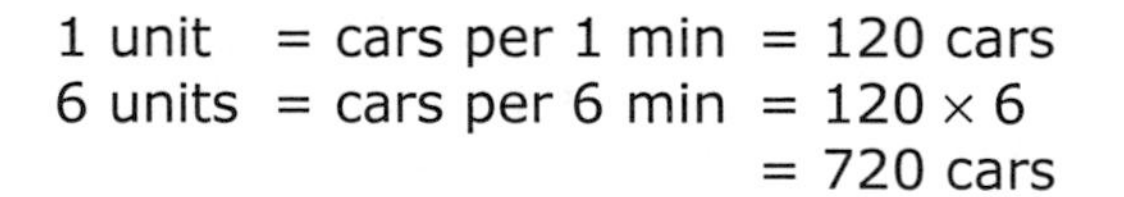

   - Now, tell students that while we can use bar diagrams for helping us determine whether to divide or multiply for rate diagrams, there is a special diagram for rate problems: a line diagram.
   - Show students a line diagram for the bar diagram already on the board.
     - Explain, as you draw the diagram, that we first make a mark and label it for the rate relationship that we know: 120 cars and 1 minute. Usually we put the time on the bottom.
     - Then, we make another mark for the relationship that has an unknown value: The number of cars in 6 minutes. Since 6 minutes is greater than 1 min, we know to mark 6 min to the right of the first mark. We label the mark with "? cars" for the unknown number of cars.

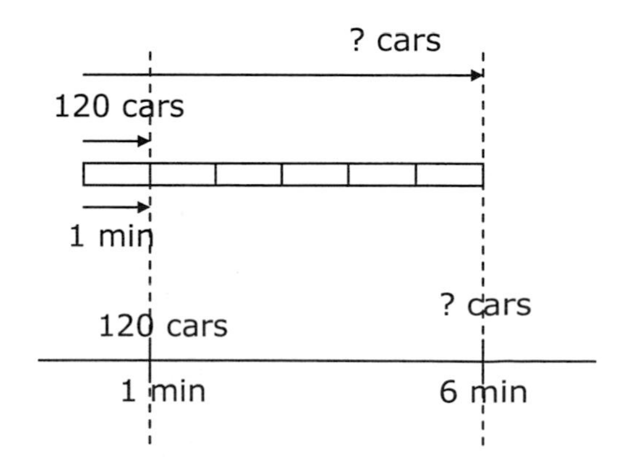

- Why are we interested in a line diagram, when the bar diagram worked fine? Suppose the question had been to find the number of cars the machine will make in 30 minutes. Drawing 30 bars for 30 1-minute units would be laborious. With a line diagram, all we need is a line and two marks for the four values in the rate problem, the three we know and the one we need to find. In later grades, we will have more difficult problems, where a line diagram will be needed.
    - Draw the line diagram.
    - Tell students that looking at the line diagram tells us that we can find the corresponding value at the 30 minute mark by multiplying the value at the 1 minute mark (120) by 30.

120 cars ? cars

1 min

120 cars ? cars

1 min 30 min

- Write the two equations on the board.

Number of cars in 1 min = 120 cars
Number of cars in 30 min = 120×30
= 3600 cars

2. Discuss **task 4, textbook p. 45**.
    - Ask students to draw a line diagram for this problem. You can call on a student to come up and draw it on the board.
    - Write the equations on the board.

5 flashes ? flashes

1 min 30 min

Number of flashes in 1 min = 5 flashes
Number of flashes in 30 min = 5×30
= 150 flashes

3. Discuss additional line diagrams.
    - Guide students in creating a line diagram for **task 1, textbook p. 45**.
        - Lead students to see that they should first label one mark for $20 and 4 hours, since that is the relationship given in the problem. Then, since they are asked for the amount paid per hour, i.e. the amount of pay for 1 hour, they would label a second mark to the left of the first one to show 1 hour and "? dollars".

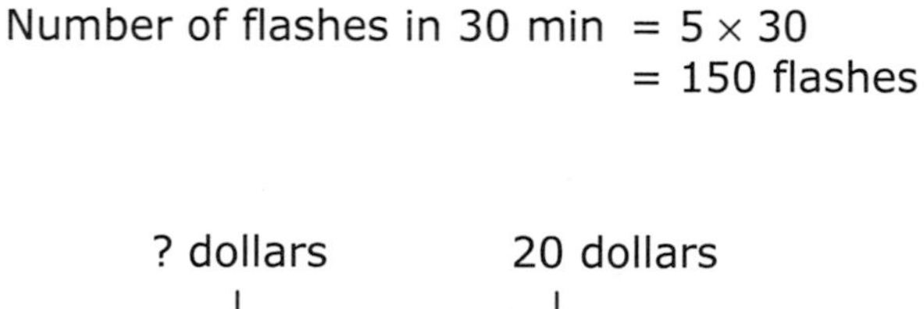

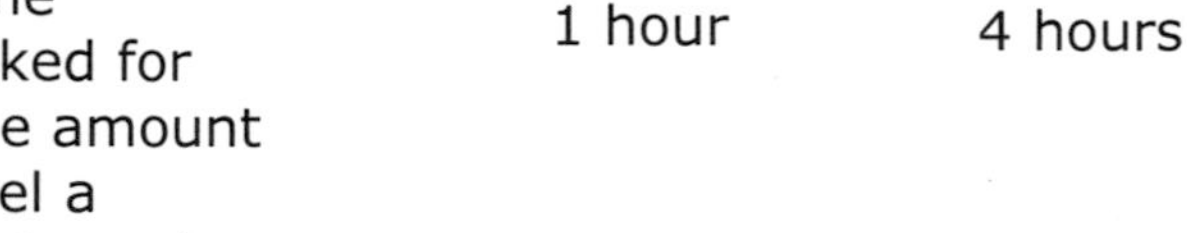

- Have students make a line diagram for **task 2, textbook p. 45**, and for the problem on p. 44 of the textbook.
- You can also have students make line diagrams for the problems in workbook Exercises 31 (c) and (d) and Workbook Exercise 32, if there is time, or have them do it for homework.

Workbook Exercise 32

Activity 4.1c **Arrows and rate problems**

1. Introduce using arrows for rate problems.
   - Write the problem shown here on the board. This is a rate problem, involving the rate as number of dollars earned per hour

     > Anna makes $5 an hour babysitting. How much does she make in 3 hours?

     - Tell students this is a simple problem that can easily be solved mentally, but we will use it to introduce some new methods that will commonly be used for harder problems and problems with larger numbers.
     - Ask students for the two quantities and how they relate to each other (5 dollars per 1 hour). Ask them for the new correspondence we want to find (the number of dollars for 3 hours).
     - Have students tell you how to draw line diagram on the board, or call on students to draw it on the board.

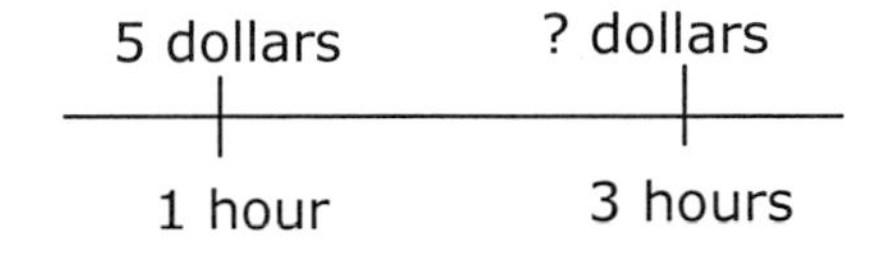

     - Write the two equations, one for each rate.

Number of dollars in 1 hr = $5
Number of dollars in 3 hr = $\$5 \times 3 = \$15$

     - Point out that while we can write "Number of dollars in 1 h = $5", it is not correct to write 1 h = $5, because hours and dollars are different measures.
     - So that we don't have to write out everything, we can use arrows to show the relationship between the two quantities.
     - Write the arrow "equations" on the board.

$1 \text{ h} \longrightarrow \$5$
$3 \text{ h} \longrightarrow \$5 \times 3 = \$15$

     - Tell students that the first arrow says, "1 h pay is $5".
     - Anna works 3 hours, which is 1 h multiplied by 3, so her pay is also multiplied by 3.
     - Point out that the two quantities we know, hours, go to the left side of the arrow. We don't know all the dollar values, so dollars go to the right of the arrows.
     - Point out that we are doing the same thing to the values on both sides of the arrow. To go from 1 h to 3 h, we multiply by 3. So we multiply $5 by 3.

$\times 3$ ($1 \text{ h} \longrightarrow \$5$) $\times 3$
$3 \text{ h} \longrightarrow \$5 \times 3 = \$15$

   - Write the problem shown here on the board.

     > A machine makes 1800 cans of soda pop in 1 day (24 hours). How many cans does it make in 1 hour?

     - Ask students to draw a line diagram to represent the information in the problem.
     - Remind students that line diagrams are an easy way to organize the information in rate problems, since they show the exact relationships between the quantities given in the problem, and the one that must be found.

- Ask students to draw a line diagram and guide them in solving the problem, using arrows to show the relationship between the quantities.
- Point out that to go from 24 hours to 1 hour, we divide by 24, so we also divide 1800 cans by 24, and this lets us find the number of cans made in 1 hour.
- Tell students that it is a good time to get into the practice of writing division as fractions. In many cases they will be able to simplify the fraction before dividing. In this case, if they simplify the fraction, they avoid dividing by 24.

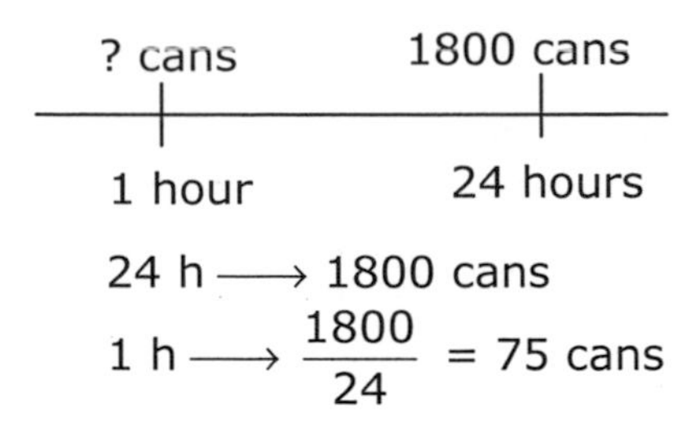

- Write the problem shown here on the board.

> Water drips from a tap at the rate of 2 liters per minute. How long will it take for 12 liters to drip out?

  - Tell students that although they can probably solve this problem mentally, you want them to see how to solve it using line diagrams and arrows. In this problem, the unknown is minutes, so students will be finding the time needed for 1 liter to drip out, rather than trying to use liters per minute.
  - Draw a line for the line diagram and let students tell you how to label it.

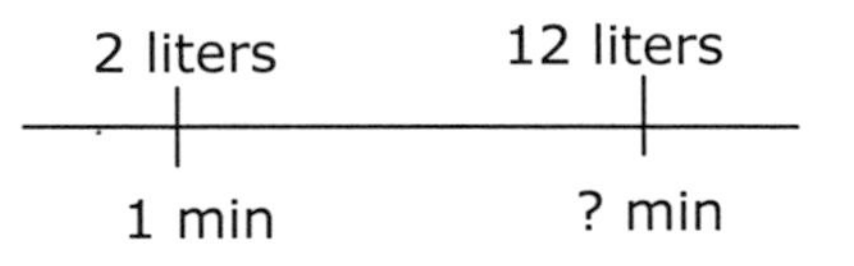

  - Draw an arrow to show the known relationship: 2 liters for 1 min. Tell students that since we know the number of liters (12) for the new minutes (?) we want to find, we put liters first, to the left of the arrow, and minutes on the right of the arrow. If we find the number of minutes for 1 liter, we can find it for any number of liters.

$2\ \ell \longrightarrow 1$ min

  - Guide students in solving first for 1 liter.
  - Point out that we are doing the same thing to the numbers on both sides of the arrow.
  - When we divide one by 2 (going from 2 liters to 1 liter), we also divide the minutes on the other side by 2.
  - This step finds the rate, in minutes per liter.

$1\ \ell \longrightarrow \frac{1}{2}$ min

  - Now, we look for the time it takes for 12 liters to drip out. To go from 1 liter to 12 liters we multiply by 12, so we also multiply the number of minutes by 12.

$12\ \ell \longrightarrow \frac{1}{2} \times 12$ min

$= 6$ min

  - Tell students that, in this particular problem, we could have solved the problem more easily. Since 12 liters is 6 times as much as 2 liters, then we could simply multiply the number of minutes by 6. Show this on the board with two arrows.

$2\ \ell \longrightarrow 1$ min

$12\ \ell \longrightarrow ?$

$= 2 \times 6$ min

- Write the problem shown here on the board. This problem is similar to the previous example, but students are less likely to be able to solve it mentally, or just "know" the answer.
  - Ask students to use a line diagram and arrows to solve this problem.
  - Have them share their solutions.
  - Point out that we know the two values for the number of pages, so we put pages to the left of the arrows, and find the number of minutes for 1 page.
  - Emphasize that, in finding the time it takes to copy 1 page, you are finding a rate in minutes per page ($\frac{1}{24}$ minutes per page).

> A photocopier can print 24 pages per minute. How long does it take to print 2064 pages?

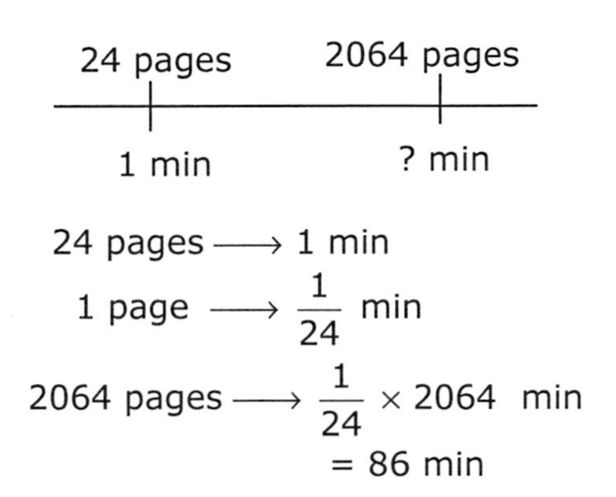

2. Discuss **tasks 5-6, textbook p. 46**.
   - Make sure students can relate the information on the line model to the information given in the problem and understands how the arrows show the relationships given in the line diagram.
   - In task 5(b), we need to find a new number of minutes, so we put minutes to the right of the arrow. We first find how long it takes to fill 1 gallon by using division, then how long it takes to fill 100 gallons by using multiplication.
     - Point out that we don't have to first find $\frac{1}{25} = 0.04$ before going on to the second step. It can be easier to simplify ($\frac{1}{\cancel{25}_1} \times \cancel{100}^4 = 4$) than divide to get a decimal.
     - Ask students if they see a short-cut. 100 gallons is 4 times as much as 25 gallons, so we can simply multiply the time it takes to fill 25 gallons (1 min) by 4.

$$\times 4 \left(\begin{array}{l} 25 \text{ gal} \longrightarrow 1 \text{ min} \\ 100 \text{ gal} \longrightarrow ? \\ \qquad\qquad = 1 \times 4 \text{ min} \end{array} \right) \times 4$$

   - In task 6, the rate is 45 words, but we need to find the rate of minutes per word, since we have to find the minutes (? min) for a new number of words (135). We put words to the left of the arrow when showing the given relationship between words and minutes (24 words in 1 minute). Then, we find the number of minutes for 1 word (the rate minutes per word). Once we know this, we can find how long it takes to type any number of words.
     - Point out that we don't want to find the value for $\frac{1}{45}$ first. Let students try this; it is a repeating decimal.
     - If we notice that 135 words is 3 times as much as 45 words, we could solve the problem by simply multiplying 1 min by 3.

Workbook Exercise 33

Activity 4.1d **Rate problems**

1. Discuss **tasks 7-8, textbook p. 47**.
   - In task 7, we are given the distance traveled, 96 km, and told that can be done on 8 liters of gas. Then we are asked for the rate. Before finding the rate, have students read Task 7(a) and look at the line diagram.
     - Since we will need to find the number of kilometers for a new number of liters, we will first find it for 1 liter. So liters go to the left of the arrow.
     - The first arrow shows the given relationship; 96 kilometers for 1 liter.
     - Then we find the number of kilometers for 1 liter, shown with the next arrow. This is the rate, which is the answer to the first question.
     - Now that we know how far the car can travel on 1 liter of gas (12 km), we can find how far it can travel on 15 liters of gas. This is shown with the third arrow.
   - In 7(b), we are given the change in kilometers, and need to find the new amount for liters, so we put liters on the right-hand side of the arrow.

2. Have students do **problems 1-6, Practice 4A, textbook p. 50**, and call on some of them to explain their solutions. Allow any who have an alternate solution to explain theirs as well.

Workbook Exercise 34

Activity 4.1e **Rate tables**

1. Discuss rate tables.
   - Discuss **task 9, textbook p. 48**.
   - Once this problem has been solved, tell students that this is a rate table.
   - Discuss another problem using the same rate table:
     - Ask students what the total parking fee would be for if the car had been parked there from 3:30 pm to 7:30 pm.
     - The fee from 3:30 to 5:00 is $1 for each half hour. There are 3 half hours, so the fee for that portion of the time is $3. From 5:00 pm to 7:30 pm is two and a half hour. The fee is $1 per hour. So the fee for that time would be $3, because any portion of an hour after 5:00 pm costs $1.
     - The fee is $1 from 7:00 to 8:00, no matter what time the car leaves between 7:00 and 8:00. So any portion of the next hour costs another $1. The rate goes up on steps, not continuously.

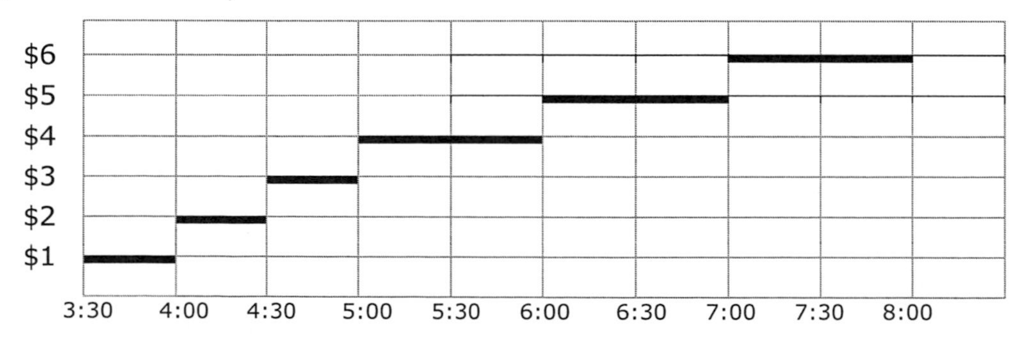

   - Have students find the parking fees for other durations at different times of the day.
   - Discuss other places where rate charges might be used, as with postal charges. If you have a scale, they can weigh paper filled envelopes or magazines and calculate the postage.

2. Discuss **tasks 10-12, textbook pp. 48-49**.
   - For task 10, also have student calculate the pay for working other days of the week.
   - For task 11, also have students calculate the postal charges for other weights.
   - For task 12, also have student calculate the taxi fares for some other distances.

3. Have students do **problems 7-8, Practice 4A, textbook p. 50**.

   Workbook Exercise 35

Activity 4.1f **Practice**

1. Since rate is a new concept for many students, you may want to do some activities where students find some rates from actual measurements. Students can work in groups. For example:
   - Students can measure how fast they can do some activity in a minute, such as writing their names over and over for 30 seconds, counting how many repetitions they did, and then finding the rate for 1 minute. Make a table of these for the class. Students have different writing rates and different name lengths so they can compare the rates.
   - If you have a computer in your class room, students can find their typing speed by typing a given passage for a set amount of time using a word processing program that determines word count, or timing how long it takes to type the passage. Use the word count feature of the program to find the number of characters including spaces in the passage, and divide it by 5 to find the number of words (most typing programs use 5 characters per word). Then find the rate of words per minute.

2. Have students solve some of the following problems, and share their solutions.
   - A machine can make 480 toys in an hour. How many toys can it make in 15 minutes? (120 toys)
   - It takes 10 hours for a carpenter to make 5 chairs. How long will it take him to make 182 chairs? (364 hours)
   - A machine can produce 65 cans of soda in 4 minutes. How long will it take to produce 1300 cans? (80 minutes)
   - A wheel makes $\frac{1}{3}$ revolution in one second. How long does it take to make 1000 revolutions? (3000 seconds, or 50 minutes)
   - Sara saves 35¢ a day. How many days will she take to save at least $10? (29 days)
   - A photocopier can print 16 pages a minute. How long will it take to print 9 copies of a document that is 256 pages long? (144 min or 2 h 24 min)
   - Water flows into an empty tank at the rate of 8 liters per minute. The water leaks out at the rate of 250 ml per minute. How much water is there in the tank after 2 hours? (930 liters)
   - The rate for telephone calls to another country is $12.50 for the first block of 3 minutes, and $1.80 for each subsequent block of 30 seconds. How much does Jasmine have to pay for an $8\frac{1}{4}$ minute call to this country? ($32.30) If she has $31.00 for a telephone call to her aunt in this country, what was the longest Jasmine could talk to her aunt? (8 min)
   - The special group rate for a cruise is $450 per person for the first and second adult, $250 per person for the third and fourth adult, and $275 per person for children 11 years old or younger. Mr. Sandor went on a cruise with his mother, wife, and four children aged 5, 8, 10, and 16 years old. How much did he pay for the family? ($2225)

Unit 5 – Graphs

Objectives

- Read and interpret data in a line graph.
- Solve problems using data given in a line graph.

Suggested number of sessions: 4

	Objectives	Textbook	Workbook	Activities
Part 1 : Line Graphs				**4 sessions**
41	▪ Understand the relationship between the data in a table and the data in a line graph. ▪ Read and interpret data in a line graph.	p. 51		5.1a
42	▪ Solve problems using data given in a line graph.	p. 52, tasks 1-2	Ex. 36	5.1b
43	▪ Construct a line graph.			5.1c
44	▪ Understand and use conversion graphs.	p. 53, task 3	Ex. 37	5.1d

Part 1: Line Graphs — 4 sessions

Objectives

- Read and interpret line graphs.
- Solve problems using data presented in line graphs.
- Solve problems using data presented in a conversion graph.

Materials

- Copies of pages 66 and 67 of this guide
- Examples of line graphs from other subjects
- Graph paper

Homework

- Workbook Exercise 36
- Workbook Exercise 37

Notes

In earlier levels of *Primary Mathematics*, students learned to interpret picture graphs and bar graphs. Here they will learn about line graphs as another form of data representation.

The *line graphs* in this section display data measurements collected over a period of time. The time at which the measurement was made is marked along one axis of the graph, while the other axis indicates the specific measurement obtained. That is, individually measured data points are graphed to also indicate the time at which the measurement was made. For visual convenience, the data points are connected by lines drawn between successive data points. From the line graph, we can immediately see the increase or decrease, over time, in the value of the measured quantity.

Unlike a line graph composed of individually measured data points, a *conversion line graph* displays a specific linked relationship between two quantities. It shows exact values for any data point; if we know the value of any one quantity, the graph lets us find the value of the other, corresponding quantity. For example, the chart on p. 53 of the textbook is marked for the relationship of two kinds of dollars: Singapore dollars to US dollars. But because the chart gives precise values, this also would let us read the values to the half dollar.

If you had students record high and low temperatures during the unit on averages, you can give the students graph paper and use this data to have students construct a line graph with three lines; the high temperatures for each day, the low temperatures for each day, and the average temperature for each day.

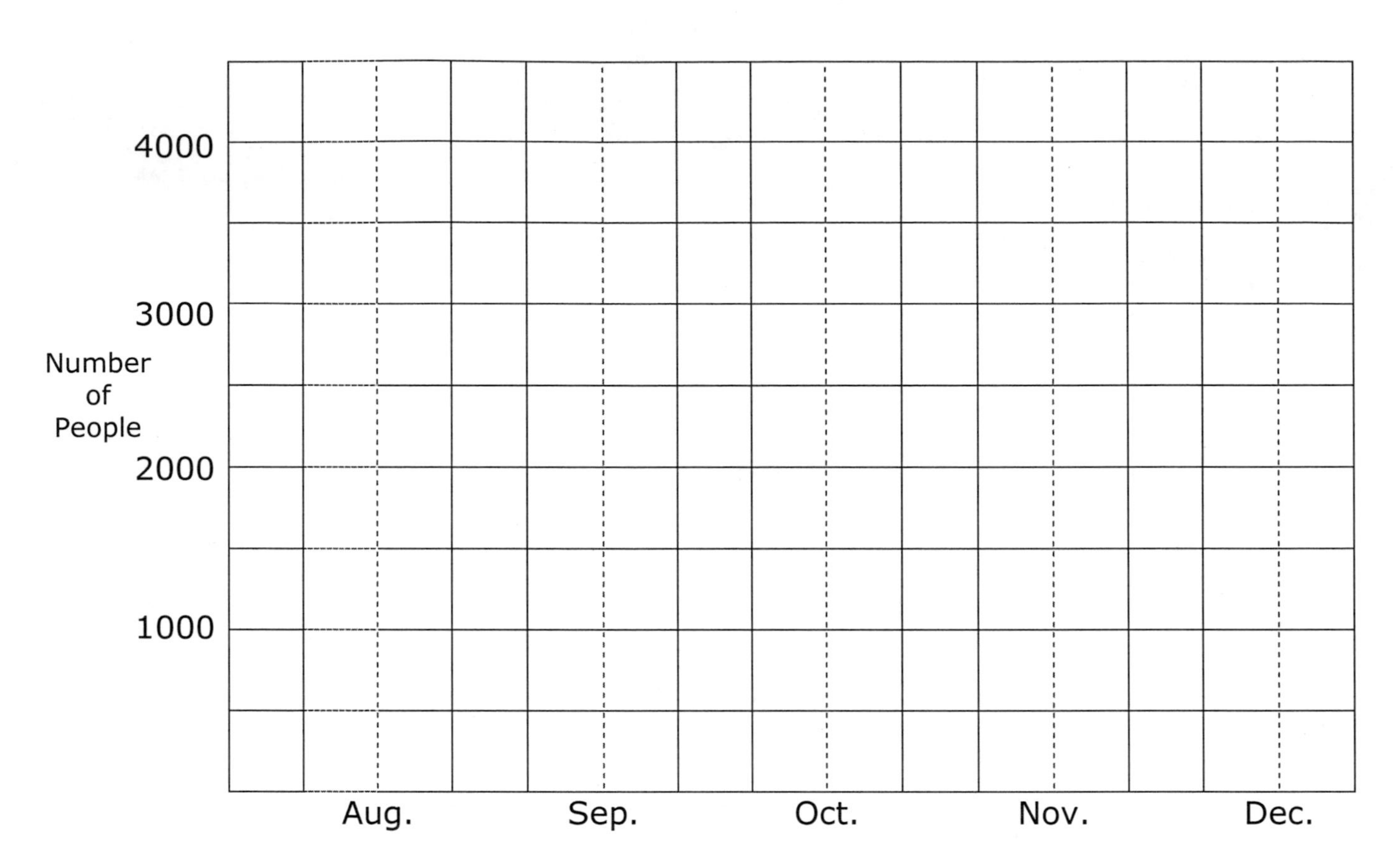
Graph for Attendance at a Swimming Pool
4000
3000
2000
1000
Number of People
Aug.
Sep.
Oct.
Nov.
Dec.

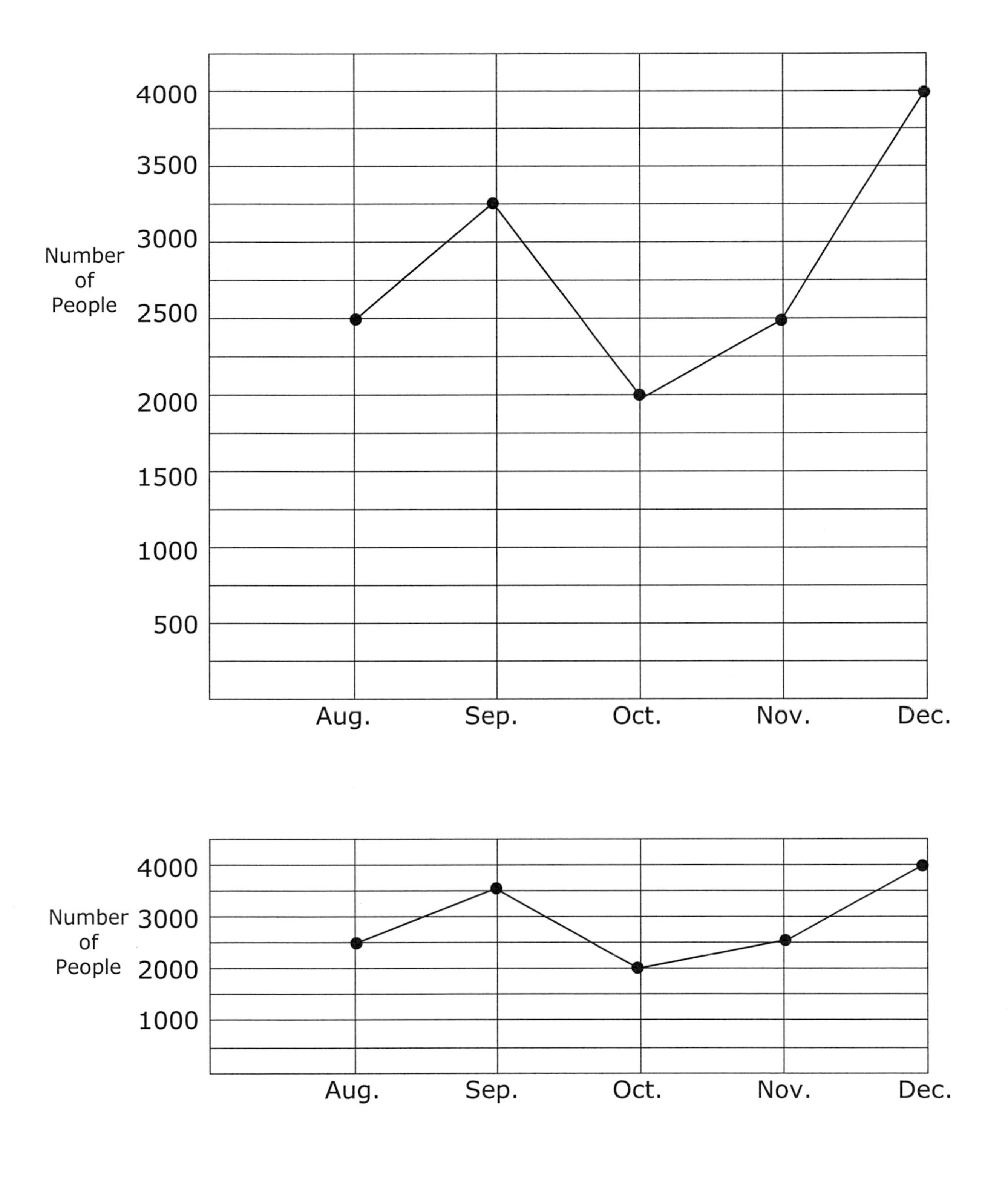
4000
3500
3000
Number
of
People
2500
2000
1500
1000
500
Aug.
Sep.
Oct.
Nov.
Dec.
4000
Number
of
People
3000
2000
1000
Aug.
Sep.
Oct.
Nov.
Dec.

Activity 5.1a **Line graphs**

1. Introduce line graphs.
   - Remind students that graphs are a way of presenting data. They have seen bar graphs before. You may want to review some of the material from unit 4 in *Primary Mathematics 4A*.
   - Copy the table on **p. 51 of the textbook** onto the board.
   - Tell students that this data comes from a swimming pool in Singapore.
   - Distribute copies of p. 66 of this guide to the students.
   - Guide students in drawing a bar graph for the data in the table, making each bar two columns wide.
   - Discuss the bar graph.
     - Each bar shows the attendance for one particular month.
     - Point out that every second horizontal line is labeled in thousands, so each line across marks 500 people. This is the scale of the graph.
   - Tell students that besides a bar graph, there is another way to graph data, called a line graph.
   - Have students draw a dot in the middle of the top of each bar. That one dot, by itself, actually indicates the same information as the bar. It marks the intersection of the vertical line, indicating the month, and the horizontal line, giving the attendance.
   - Have students connect the dots with a line.
   - Have them compare their graphs to the graph on **p. 51 of the textbook**.
   - The dots, which are the data points showing us the data that was collected, are connected by straight lines, drawn from one point to the next. This type of graph is called a line graph.
   - Discuss why a line graph might be useful.
     - Each bar of a bar graph represents an equivalent data point on the line graph. The bar graph makes the value of each bar easy to find. The value of a particular data point in the line graph is a little harder to find, but the lines which connect the points emphasize the relationship between adjacent data points.

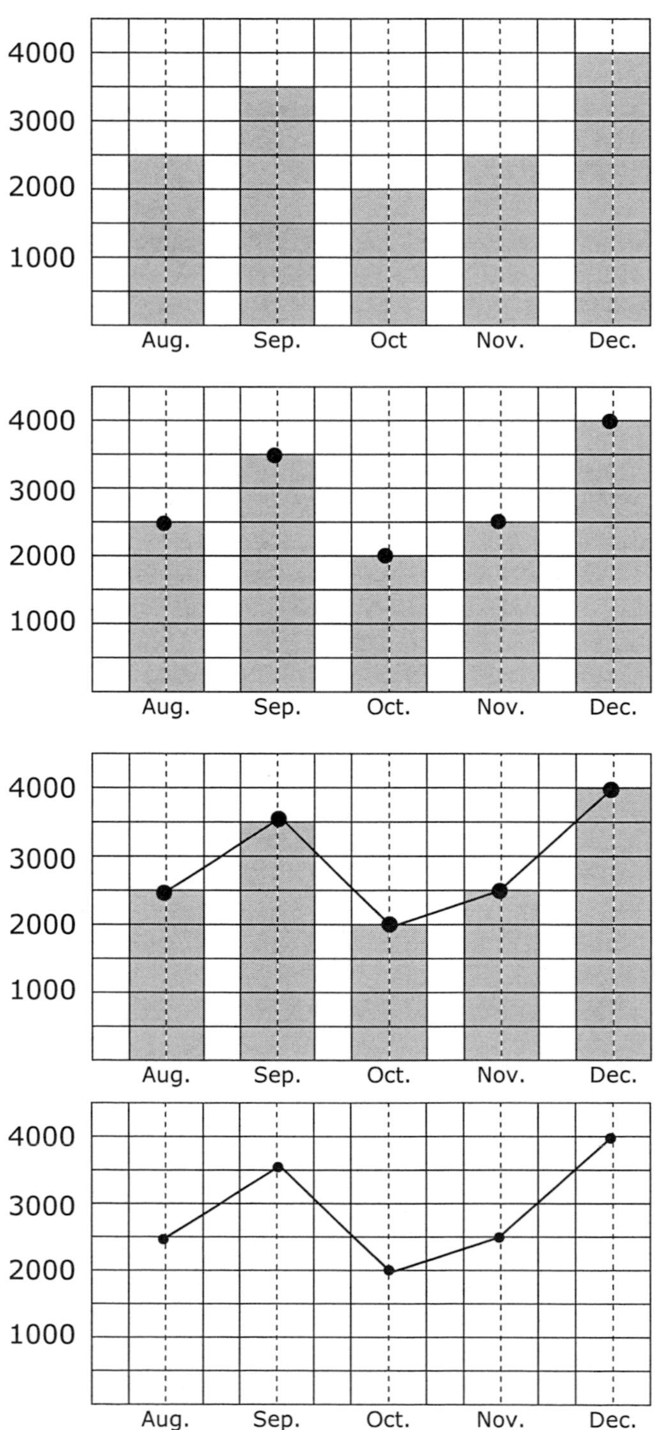

  - The line graph helps us to easily see the increase and decrease of data from one time to the next. If the line goes up, there was an increase, and if it goes down, there was a decrease.
- Have students answer the questions in (a)-(c).
  - Point out that questions (a) and (b) are easily answered with the line graph. For question (c), we need to find the exact values. If the points on the graph don't line up exactly with the numbers on the scale, it is better to use the values in a table.
  - Tell students that in Singapore the school year goes from January to December, with a month break in June and December. Ask them to use this information and the graph to predict attendance at the pool in January.

2. Discuss scale.
   - Tell students that, when interpreting line graphs, it is important to look at the scale being used.
   - Distribute copies of p. 67 of this guide.
   - Tell students that these graphs both contain the same information as the graph on p. 51 of the textbook.
   - Ask them which graph might be used by someone who wanted to convince readers that there was a considerable increase in attendance at the pool in December. Which graph would someone use who might want to convince readers that there was not much variation in pool attendance from month to month?
   - Misleading graphs are often used in advertisement and politics. It is important to examine data to determine if they really support the claims being made.

3. You may want to ask students to find some line graphs in newspapers, magazines, or textbooks to bring in for the next class.

Activity 5.1b **Interpret line graphs**

1. Discuss **tasks 1-2, textbook p. 52**.
   - Point out that in task 1, we do not know the exact number of people shopping at any particular time. The data measured was the number of people coming into the store during one hour. For example, the 5 p.m. data point marks the total number of people that came into the store between 4 p.m. and 5 p.m.

2. Display line graphs from various sources and discuss any information that can be derived from them and possible reasons for any trends that might be observed.
   - In particular, draw students' attention to the scale of the axes and discuss whether the scale used for the graph helps a reader to draw the conclusion that the author is using the graph to illustrate. Point out that in interpreting graphs, we can't just look at the line and how steep it is, but we also have to look at the actual numbers and the scale.

Workbook Exercise 36

Activity 5.1c **Construct a line graph**

1. Construct a line graph.
   - If students have been recording high and low temperatures over a period of days, as suggested for Unit 3, you can guide your students in drawing line graphs for this data. Provide them with graph paper and help them determine appropriate scales for the axes.
   - If students haven't been recording the temperatures, provide them with other data to graph.

Activity 5.1d **Conversion graphs**

1. Discuss **task 3, textbook p. 53**.
   - Tell students that this is a *conversion graph*, also called a *rate graph*. You may want to discuss exchange rates.
     - If someone from the U.S., for example, goes to another country, they can go to a bank and exchange some of the U.S. money for money used in the country they are visiting. The *exchange rate* tells them, and the banker, what a U.S. dollar is worth in the local currency.
     - If we are told that 1 U.S. dollar can be exchanged for 2 Singapore dollars, for example, we can find how many Singapore dollars we would get for a certain number of U.S. dollars (or vice versa) using rate calculations.
     - We can also use a rate graph, such as the one shown on p. 53.
   - Guide students in using the graph to answer the questions on this page.
   - Point out that for this kind of graph, the information is *continuous* between the points shown on this graph. We could use it to find how many Singapore dollars can be exchanged for a value that does not have a point on the graph, such as $2.50.
   - Ask students whether they think it is easier to use a conversion graph or rate calculations. For amounts between the lines on a graph, we would have to estimate the exchange, particularly if the conversion graph is not as simple as a 2 to 1 rate. Calculations would give us a more accurate answer.

1 \$US $\longrightarrow$ 2 \$S
15 \$US $\longrightarrow$ 2 x 15 = 30 \$S

2 \$S $\longrightarrow$ 1 \$US
15 \$S $\longrightarrow$ $\frac{1}{2}$ x 15 = 7.50 \$US

Workbook Exercise 37

Review B

Objectives

- Review all topics.

Suggested number of sessions: 2

	Objectives	Textbook	Workbook	Activities
Review A				**2 sessions**
45 46	▪ Review.	pp. 54-56, Review B		R.b

Activity R.b **Review**

1. Have students do any problems in **Review B, textbook pp. 54-56.**
   - Students should share their solutions, particularly for the word problems. Possible solutions involving models for some problems are shown here.
   - You may want to save problem 22 on p. 56 of the textbook for the beginning of Unit 6 as a review of angle properties of intersecting lines.

3. 2 units = 120
   1 unit = 120 ÷ 2 = 60
   green = 1 unit = 60
   There are 60 green paper clips.

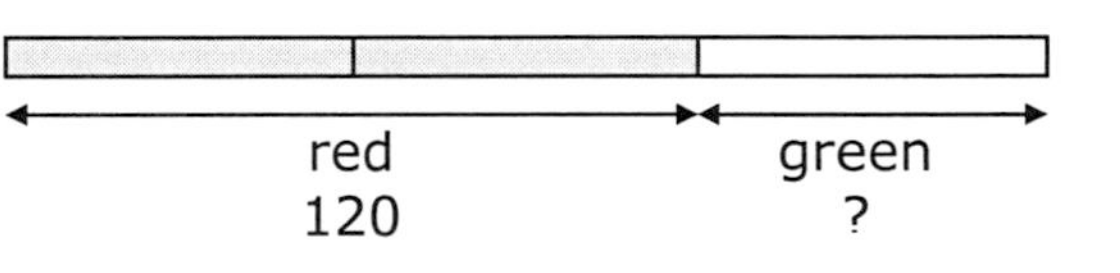

5. His salary is 5 units. He gives 1 unit to his wife.
   He spends $\frac{3}{4}$ of the remainder, or 3 units.
   5 units = \$2500
   1 unit = \$2500 ÷ 5 = \$500
   3 units = $\$500 \times 3$ = \$1500
   He spends \$1500.

\$2500
wife
remainder
amount spent

6. Total units = 1 + 3 + 4 = 8
   8 units = 96 cm
   1 unit = 96 ÷ 8 = 12 cm
   Longest rod = 4 units
   4 units = 12×4 = 48 cm

96
?

7. Carlos' [Salleh's] money is 1 unit.
   Total money = 5 units + \$5.00
   1 unit = \$2.50
   Total money = $(5 \times \$2.50)$ + \$5.00
   = \$12.50 + \$5.00
   = \$17.50

US ed. \$2.50 3d ed.
Carlos Salleh
Tom Tom
Ryan Raju
\$5.00

18. 20 ℓ ⟶ 1 min
    1 ℓ ⟶ $\frac{1}{20}$ min
    800 ℓ ⟶ $\frac{1}{20} \times 800$ min = 40 min
    It will take 40 min to fill the pool with 800 ℓ.

Unit 6 – Triangles

Objectives

- Identify right, isosceles, and equilateral triangles.
- Learn and use angle properties of a triangle:
  - The sum of the angles of a triangle is 180°.
  - The sum of the angles opposite the right angle of a right triangle is 90°.
  - The exterior angle of a triangle is equal to the sum of the opposite interior angles.
  - The base angles of an isosceles triangle are equal.
  - The angles of an equilateral triangle are 60°.
- Construct a triangle when given the measurement of two angles and the included side, or of two sides and the included angle.

Suggested number of sessions: 7

	Objectives	Textbook	Workbook	Activities
Part 1 : Sum of Angles of a Triangle				**3 sessions**
47	▪ Recognize that the sum of the angles of a triangle is 180°.	p. 57 p. 58, task 1	Ex. 38	6.1a
	▪ Find an unknown angle of a triangle when given the other two angles.	p. 58, tasks 2-3		
48	▪ Recognize that the sum of the angles opposite a right angle of a triangle is 90°.	p. 59, task 4	Ex. 39	6.1b
	▪ Find the unknown angle of a right triangle when the other angle is given.	p. 59, tasks 5-6		
49	▪ Recognize that the exterior angle of a triangle is equal to the sum of the opposite interior angles.	p. 60, task 7	Ex. 40	6.1c
	▪ Find an unknown angle in problems involving exterior angles of a triangle.	p. 60, tasks 8-9		
Part 2 : Isosceles and Equilateral Triangles				**3 sessions**
50	▪ Explore angle and side properties of isosceles and equilateral triangles.	p. 61 p. 62, tasks 1-2		6.2a
51	▪ Find unknown angles in isosceles and equilateral triangles.	pp. 62-63, task 3-5	Ex. 41 Ex. 42	6.2b
52	▪ Find an unknown angle from the angle properties of triangles.	p. 64, tasks 6-8	Ex. 43	6.2c
Part 3 : Drawing Triangles				**1 sessions**
53	▪ Construct a triangle, given the measurement of two angles and the included side. ▪ Construct a triangle, given the measurements of two sides and their included angle.	p. 65 pp. 66-67, task 1-3	Ex. 44	6.3a

Part 1: Sum of Angles of a Triangle — 3 sessions

Objectives

- Recognize that the sum of the angles of a triangle is 180°.
- Find an unknown angle of a triangle given the other two angles.
- Recognize that the sum of the angles opposite the right angle of a right triangle is 90°.
- Find an unknown angle of a right triangle given one other angle.
- Recognize that the exterior angle of a triangle is equal to the sum of the opposite interior angles.

Materials

- Protractors
- Paper for cut-out triangles
- Scissors
- Set squares (plastic triangles with a right angle)

Homework

- Workbook Exercise 38
- Workbook Exercise 39
- Workbook Exercise 40

Notes

In Primary Mathematics 5A, students learned angle properties of intersecting lines.

$\angle a = \angle c \quad \angle b = \angle d$

Vertically opposite angles are equal.

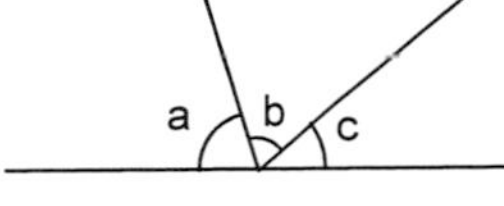

$\angle a + \angle b + \angle c = 180°$

The sum of the angles on a straight line is 180°.

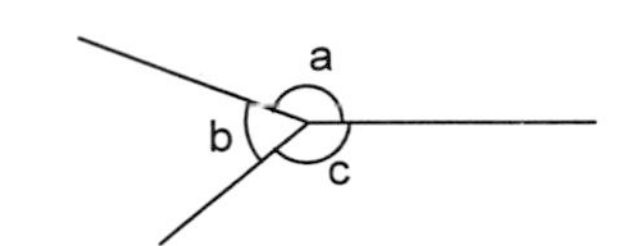

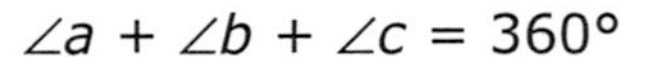

$\angle a + \angle b + \angle c = 360°$

The sum of the angles at a point is 360°.

They also learned that the sum of the angles formed by lines intersecting with a right angle is 90°.

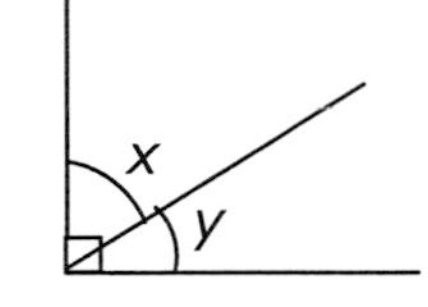

$\angle x + \angle y = 90°$

In this section, students will be introduced to the angle properties of a triangle, which are:

- The sum of the three angles of any triangle is 180°.
- When one angle of a triangle is a right angle, the other two angles add up to 90°.
- If a side of a triangle is extended, the angle it forms with the adjacent side is called an exterior angle.
- The exterior angle of a triangle is equal to the sum of the interior opposite angles of the triangle.
- Students will use these properties to find unknown angles in figures involving triangles.

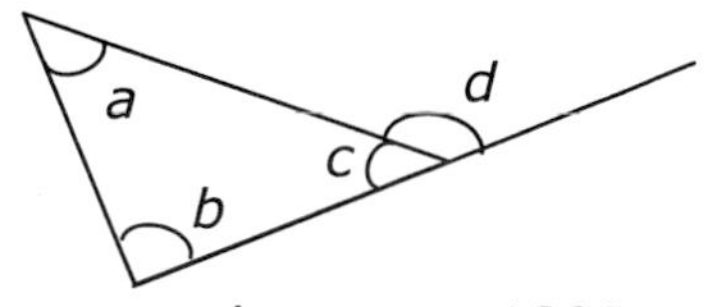

$\angle a + \angle b + \angle c = 180°$
If $\angle b$ is a right angle, then $\angle a + \angle c = 90°$
$\angle d = \angle a + \angle b$

Activity 6.1a **Angle sum of a triangle**

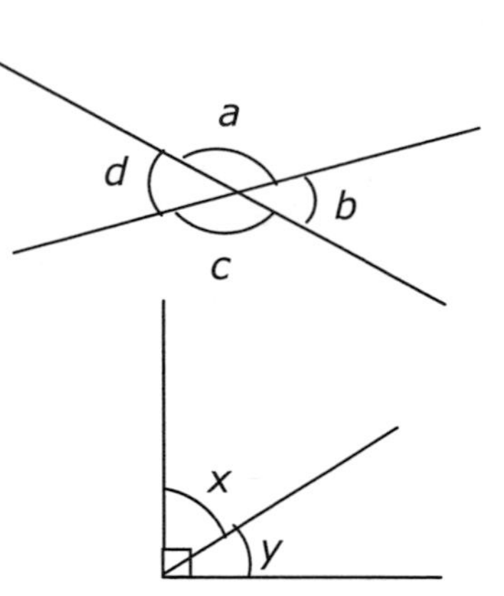

1. Review angle properties of intersecting lines.
   - Draw two intersecting lines on the board and label the angles *a*, *b*, *c*, and *d* in order, clockwise.
   - Ask students for any angle properties that they can remember. Then sum up:
     - ➢ Vertically opposite angles are equal.
     - ➢ The sum of the angles on a straight line is 180°.
     - ➢ The sum of the angles at a point is 360°.
   - Now, draw a right angle and another line which intersect it and ask students for the angle property:
   - ➢ The sum of the angles formed by lines intersecting within a right angle is 90°.
   - Have students do **problem 24, Review A, textbook p. 24**, and **problem 22, Review B, textbook p. 56**.

2. Investigate the angles of triangles.
   - Refer to **p. 57 in the textbook**. Have students do this activity. They do not need to trace the triangle on this page but can use rulers to make any triangle. They should mark the angles before cutting the triangle apart, and/or be sure to cut with a wavy edge or tear instead of cut so they know which are the original angles.
   - Allow them to investigate various types of triangles to see for themselves that the three angles add up to 180° for a variety of triangles.
   - Have students do **task 1, textbook p. 58**. In addition, they may draw their own triangles and measure the angles. If you have dynamic geometry software, such as Geometer's Sketchpad®, you can demonstrate that this property holds true as you change the shape of a triangle.

3. Have students do **tasks 2-3, textbook p. 58**.
   - If we know two angles of a triangle, we can find the third angle by subtracting both from 180°.
   - Point out that when we are asked to find unknown angles, we do so by calculation, not by measuring the angles (unless we are specifically told to measure). The triangles in the textbook and workbook are not drawn to exact scale.

Workbook Exercise 38

Activity 6.1b **Angles of a right triangle**

1. Investigate the angles of a right triangle.
   - Have students do **task 4, textbook p. 59**. They can use set-squares to draw right triangles, or simply cut one out of the corner of a piece of paper by cutting a straight line from one side to the adjacent side. Let them try the activity with right triangles of different shapes and sizes.
   - Ask them if they could derive the property that the sum of the two non-right angles in a right triangle is 90° from the property that all the angles of a triangle add up to 180°. The sum of the two angles must be 180° – 90° = 90°.
   - Make sure students remember that the little square marked in the corner of a triangle (or other shape) indicates that the angle is a right angle.

2. Have students do **tasks 5-6, textbook p. 59**.
   - For task 6, point out that if two angles of a triangle add up to 90°, then the third angle is a right angle.

Workbook Exercise 39

Activity 6.1c **Exterior angle of a triangle**

1. Define the exterior angle of a triangle and find its opposite interior angles.
   - Draw a triangle on the board and extend one of its lines. Mark the interior angles as shown.
   - Point to the three angles of the triangle and tell students that these are called internal angles.
   - Now mark $\angle d$ and guide students to see that when the side is extended, a third angle ($\angle d$) was formed, called an external angle.
   - Point out that the external angle plus the internal angle next to it total 180° ($\angle c + \angle d = 180°$).
   - Tell students that the other two internal angles ($\angle a$ and $\angle b$) are referred to as opposite internal angles of the exterior $\angle d$.
   - Extend the other two sides and have students identify the external angles and their opposite internal angles.

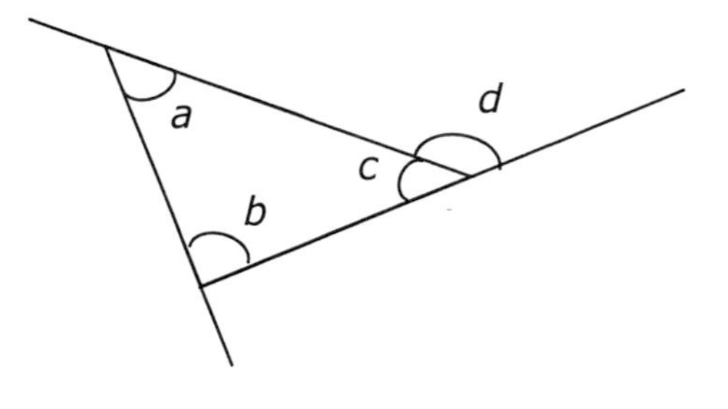

2. Investigate the relationship between the exterior angle and the opposite interior angles.
   - Have students do **task 7, textbook p. 60**
   - Give students construction paper and scissors. Ask them to make triangles of various sizes and shapes and mark the angles. Then, demonstrate how to cut or tear off the two opposite angles; and then, to lay the remaining side along the edge of a piece of paper, so they can fit the two cut angles into the exterior angle. If the angles are cut off rather than torn off, make the cut wavy, rather than straight, so that there is not confusion about which were the original angles.
   - Ask them if they could derive the property that the exterior angle of a triangle is equal to the sum of the interior opposite angles from properties that they already know. Since the sum of the interior angles is 180°, then any two of the angles is the difference between 180° and the third angle. But since the third angle and the exterior angle are on a straight line, the exterior angle is also the difference between 180° and the third angle. Therefore, the exterior angle is equal to the sum of the opposite interior angles.

$\angle a + \angle b + \angle c = 180°$
$\angle a + \angle b = 180° - \angle c$
$\angle d = 180° - \angle c$
so
$\angle a + \angle b = \angle d$

3. Have students do **tasks 8-9, textbook p. 60**.

Workbook Exercise 40

Part 2: Isosceles and Equilateral Triangles **3 sessions**

Objectives

- Identify isosceles and equilateral triangles.
- Recognize that the base angles of an isosceles triangle are equal.
- Recognize that all the angles of an equilateral triangle are 60°.
- Find an unknown angle of a triangle when given the other two angles.

Materials

- Straws or cardboard strips
- Paper cut out triangles
- Set squares (plastic triangles with one right triangle)

Homework

- Workbook Exercise 41
- Workbook Exercise 42
- Workbook Exercise 43

Notes

Triangles are classified in two ways.

1. According to angles:

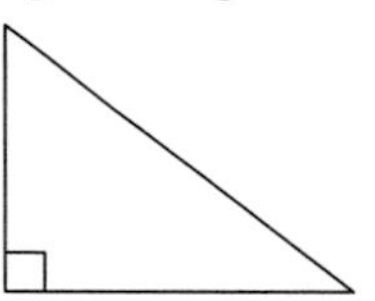

A **right-angled triangle** or **right triangle** has a right angle (90°).

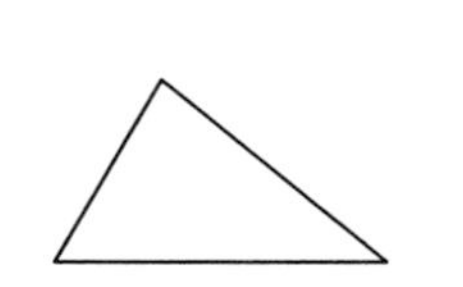

An **acute triangle** has 3 acute angles (smaller than 90°).

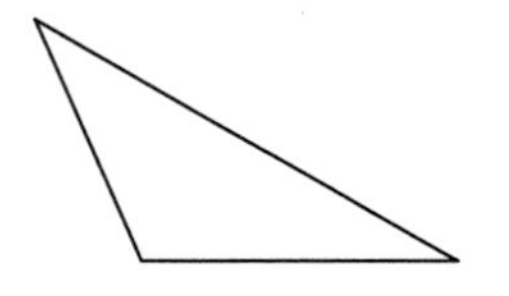

An **obtuse triangle** has one obtuse angle (greater than 90°).

2. According to sides:

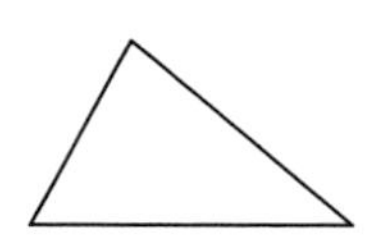

A **scalene triangle** has all sides different in length.

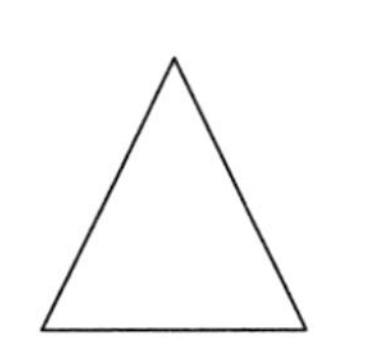

An **isosceles** triangle has two equal sides.

An **equilateral triangle** has three equal sides.

Students don't have to memorize the terms scalene, acute, and obtuse here.

In Primary Mathematics, an equilateral triangle is considered to also be an isosceles triangle. Most mathematicians use this terminology, but some school texts do not. If also using other textbooks, students should find out which convention is being used.

If a triangle is an isosceles triangle, then the two angles facing the equal sides are equal.

Conversely: If two angles of a triangle are the same, then the triangle is an isosceles triangle.

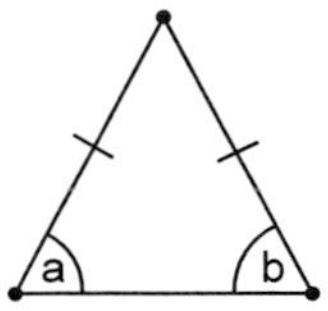

$\angle a = \angle b$

Little cross-lines on the drawing of a geometric figure indicate that the marked sides are equal in length.

A right triangle can be an isosceles triangle. The other two angles would each be 45°.

If a triangle is an equilateral triangle, then all three angles equal 60°.

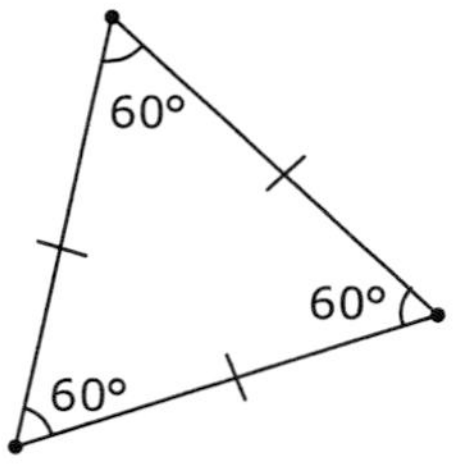

Conversely: If each of the three angles of a triangle is 60°, then the triangle is an equilateral triangle.

If we are told that two of the angles are 60°, then we know it is an equilateral triangle, because the third angle must be 60°.

Students will be finding unknown angles using all the angle properties they have learned. Do not insist that they write down the reason for each step of the calculation for finding the unknown angle. Encourage them to give the reasons during oral discussion. There can be more than one solution.

Activity 6.2a Properties of isosceles and equilateral triangles

1. Explore angles and sides of equilateral and isosceles triangles.
   - Refer to **p. 61 in the textbook**.
   - Tell students that a triangle with three equal sides is called an equilateral triangle. Write the word on the board. You may want to tell them that "equi-" means "same" or "equal" and "lateral" means "sides". So equilateral means equal sides.
   - Have students name the equilateral triangles on p. 61. (A and C)
   - Tell students that a triangle with two equal sides is called an isosceles triangle. You may want to tell them that "iso-" also means "equal" and that "sceles" comes from a word meaning "leg". So isosceles means equal legs. An isosceles triangle has two equal "legs" or sides.
   - Have students name the isosceles triangles on p. 61. (All four are isosceles triangles, but A and C are also equilateral.)
   - Provide students with straws and paperclips. The paperclips can be unbent in the middle and the two curved ends inserted into the straws to hold them together at the vertices.
   - Have students make triangles like those on p. 61, by cutting three equal lengths of straw and putting them together. Then, cut two equal lengths and a third different length, and put them together. They do not have to use the same lengths as shown on this page; different students should have different triangles.
   - Provide students with protractors. Have them trace their straw triangles on paper and see if they can determine anything about the angles. Allow students to confer to see if they can come up with a generalization. They may discover that two angles of an isosceles triangle are equal, and that all the angles of an equilateral triangle are equal. They may also find that all the angles of the equilateral triangles are 60°.
   - Have students look at **task 1, textbook p. 62**. They can do this task with their isosceles triangles.
   - Discuss **task 2, textbook p. 62**. If two angles of a triangle are equal, then the triangle is an isosceles triangle (the opposite sides are also equal).

Activity 6.2b Unknown angles in isosceles and equilateral triangles

1. Discuss finding unknown angles in isosceles and equilateral triangles.
   - Draw an equilateral triangle on the board and give the angle for one of the base angles. Mark the two sides that are equal with little cross-lines (little perpendicular lines). Remind students that this indicates which two sides are equal.
   - Ask students to find the other two angles.
   - Draw another triangle and give the angle opposite the unequal side. Ask students to find the other two angles. They need to subtract the one angle from 180°, and then divide the difference by 2, since the other two angles are the same.
   - Draw a right triangle. Ask students if a right triangle can be an isosceles triangle. It can. Label the vertices and have students tell you which sides must be equal if the right triangle is isosceles. The side opposite the right angle can never be one of the equal sides. Mark in the cross-lines.
   - Have students calculate the other two angles (45°).
   - Remind students that the drawings in the textbook and workbook are not to scale. Just because two sides may look equal does not mean that they are.

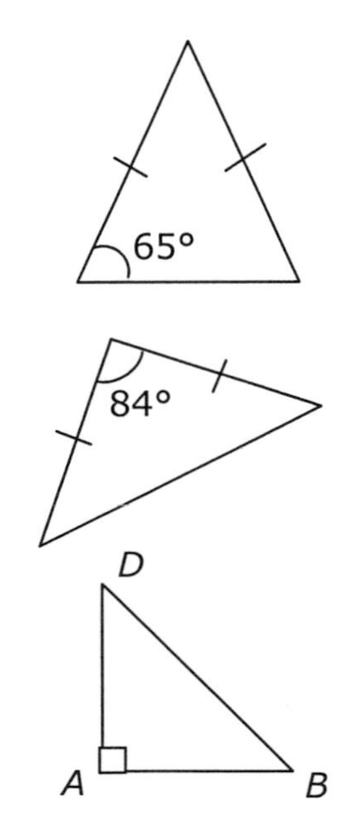

2. Discuss **tasks 3-5, textbook pp. 62-63**.
   - For task 4, point out that we only need to know two angles to determine if a triangle is equilateral. If two angles are each 60°, the third angle must also be 60°.

Workbook Exercises 41-42

Activity 6.2c **Finding unknown angles**

1. Discuss learning **tasks 6-7, textbook p. 64**.
   - In task 7, we can find ∠ACB (75°) since it is vertically opposite (and therefore equal to) ∠DCE. Since triangle ABC is isosceles, then ∠ABC = ∠ACB.
   - Point out that ∠DCE is not an external angle. Ask students to name external angles for this triangle. ∠ACD and ∠BCE are external angles.

2. Have students do **task 8, textbook p. 64**.
   - Have students share their solutions. Possible solutions are given here, as well as selected problems from the workbook exercise 43.
   - These problems often have more than one approach. Allow students to explain alternate approaches, if they have any, and discuss which method might be more efficient or make better use of angle properties.
   - Students should explain the reasoning for their steps orally, but are not required to write them down.
   - In solving these problems it is sometimes helpful to start by writing in the values of any angles that can be found using angle properties.

(a)	∠ACB = ∠CAB =50°	isosceles triangle
	∠a = 180° - 50° = 130°	angles on a straight line
(b)	∠ACB = 180° - 110° = 70°	angles on a straight line
	∠ACB = ∠CBA	isosceles triangle
	∠b = 180° - (2 x 70°) = 40°	isosceles triangle
(c)	∠ACB = 60°	equilateral triangle
	∠c = 180° - 60° = 120°	angles on a straight line
(d)	∠ACB = 60°	equilateral triangle
	∠d = 180° - 60° - 90° = 30°	adjacent ∠s on a straight line
(e)	∠BAC = ∠ACB = ∠ABC = 60°	equilateral triangle
	∠ACD = 60° + 60° = 120°	exterior ∠ of a Δ = sum of the opposite interior ∠s
	∠e = 180° - 40° - 120° = 20°	angle sum of a triangle

Workbook Exercise 43

Selected solutions:

(e)	$\angle ACB = 180° - 118° = 62°$ $\angle e = \angle ACB = 62°$	adjacent $\angle$s on a straight line isosceles triangle
(f)	$\angle DBC = 60°$ $\angle f = 180° - 60° = 120°$	equilateral triangle angles on a straight line
(g)	$\angle ACB = 60°$ $\angle g = 180° - 60° - 70° = 50°$	equilateral triangle adjacent $\angle$s on a straight line
(h)	$\angle ACB = 180° - 135° = 45°$ $\angle h = 90° - 45° = 45°$ or, $\angle h = 135° - 90° = 45°$	adjacent $\angle$s on a straight line angle sum of a triangle exterior $\angle$ of a Δ = sum of the opposite interior $\angle$s

---

Part 3: Drawing Triangles — 1 session

Objectives

- Construct a triangle, given the measurements of two angles and their included side.
- Construct a triangle, given the measurements of two sides and their included angle.

Materials

- Protractors
- Rulers
- Set-squares

Homework

- Workbook Exercise 44

Notes

Students should know how to draw angles of different sizes, and line segments of different lengths, using a protractor. They have also learned how to draw perpendicular and parallel lines using a set-square. (See p. 72 of the textbook for a picture of a set square.) If necessary, review these processes.

When a drawing of a triangle with given measurements is asked for, students might make a small sketch before drawing it full size. This can give them an idea of what the final drawing should look like, especially if they have learned to estimate angle sizes well.

Activity 6.3a **Drawing triangles**

1. Review drawing perpendicular lines and angles of a given size if necessary. Refer to Units 5 and 6 in Primary Mathematics 4B and the corresponding pages in the Teacher's Guide 4B. This can also be reviewed as you guide students through the tasks in this section of Primary Mathematics 5B.

2. Guide students through the drawing process on **p. 66 of the textbook** and in **tasks 1-2, textbook pp. 66-67**. Students can use a set-square to draw perpendicular lines.

3. Have students do **task 3, textbook p. 67**.

4. Give students the measurements (two angles and included side, or two sides and included angle) of some other triangles to draw. Ask students to first draw a small sketch of the triangle, estimating the angles, and then construct a full-scale drawing. For example:
   - Draw a triangle ABC in which AB = 7 cm, $\angle CAB = 50°$, and $\angle ABC = 54°$. Measure side AC. (5 cm).
   - Draw a triangle XYZ in which XY = 6 cm, YZ = 9 cm, and $\angle XYZ = 120°$. Measure $\angle XZY$. (24°)

Workbook Exercise 44

Unit 7 – 4-sided Figures

Objectives

- Understand and use the properties of parallelograms, rhombuses, and trapezoids.
- Find unknown angles in problems which involve quadrilaterals and triangles.
- Construct a parallelogram when given the measurement of two adjacent sides and one angle.
- Construct a rhombus when given the measurement of one side and one angle.

Suggested number of sessions: 5

	Objectives	Textbook	Workbook	Activities
Part 1 : Parallelograms, Rhombuses and Trapezoids				**3 sessions**
54	▪ Investigate properties of parallelograms, rhombuses, and trapezoids.	p. 68		7.1a
55	▪ Recognize that opposite angles of a parallelogram are equal and that the sum of the angles between parallel sides is 180°. ▪ Recognize that a diagonal bisects a rhombus (or square) into equilateral triangles. ▪ Find unknown angles in parallelograms.	pp. 69-71, tasks 1-4	Ex. 45 Ex. 46	7.1b
56	▪ Find unknown angles in problems which involve trapezoids and triangles.	p. 71, tasks 5-6	Ex. 47	7.1c
Part 2 : Drawing Parallelograms and Rhombuses				**2 sessions**
57	▪ Construct a parallelogram.	p. 72	Ex. 48, 1-2	7.2a
	▪ Construct a rectangle when given its length and width.	p. 73, task 1		
	▪ Construct a parallelogram when given the measurements of two adjacent sides and an angle.	pp. 74-75, task 2-3		
58	▪ Construct a rhombus when given the measurement of one side and one angle.	p. 75, tasks 4-5	Ex. 48, 3-4	7.2b

Part 1: Parallelograms, Rhombuses and Trapezoids — 3 sessions

Objectives

- Recognize parallelograms, rhombuses, and trapezoids.
- Recognize that rhombuses, rectangles, and squares are parallelograms.
- Learn some angle properties of parallelograms.
- Find unknown angles in problems involving parallelograms.

Materials

- Square graph paper
- Geostrips or straws and pins (or strips cut from tag-board or manila folders, a hole punch, and brads)
- Rulers
- Set-squares

Homework

- Workbook Exercise 45
- Workbook Exercise 46
- Workbook Exercise 47

Notes

Note for 3rd edition: In British English, a trapezium is a quadrilateral with one pair of parallel sides. A trapezoid is a quadrilateral having no sides parallel. In American English, the names are reversed. American English will be used in this manual.

A *quadrilateral* is a 4-sided closed figure.
A *parallelogram* is a quadrilateral with both pairs of opposite sides parallel.
A *rhombus* is a parallelogram with four equal sides.
A *trapezoid* is a quadrilateral with only one pair of parallel sides.

In *Primary Mathematics*, we follow the common definition of a trapezoid: a quadrilateral with only two sides parallel. However, the restriction that a trapezoid has only one pair of parallel sides is not yet universally used. Some texts will say a trapezoid has "at least" one pair of parallel sides, and so might refer to a parallelogram (which has two pairs of parallel lines) as a trapezoid.

The following diagram is for teacher reference:

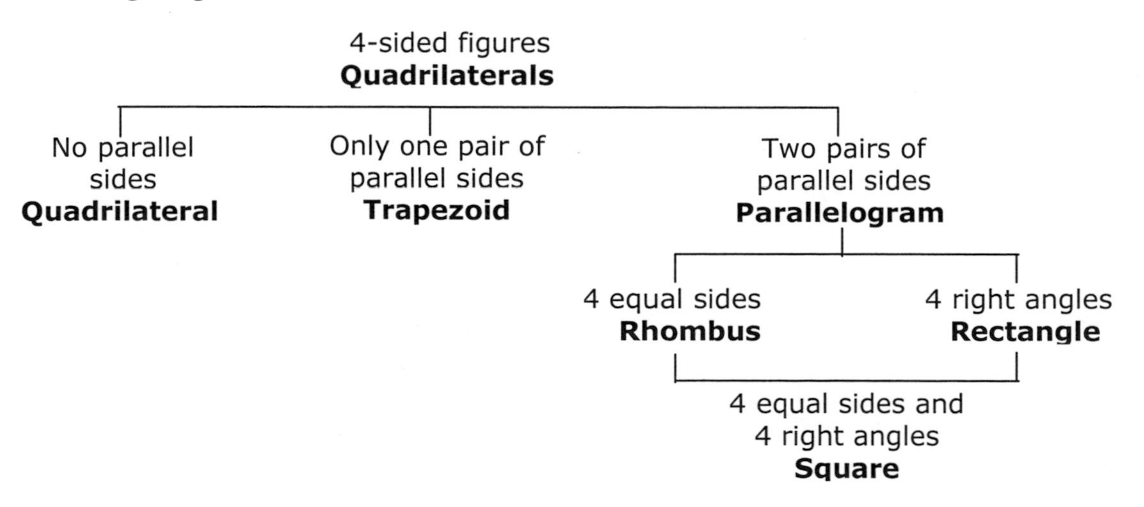

Students do not need to know all the relationships between the quadrilaterals yet, but do need to learn that rhombuses, rectangles, and squares are special parallelograms. A rectangle is a parallelogram with four right angles, a rhombus is a parallelogram with four equal sides, and a square is a parallelogram with four equal sides and four right angles. A square is therefore also a rhombus and a rectangle.

Students should learn to recognize and name parallelograms, rhombuses, and trapezoids, and know how many parallel lines each figure has.

Two angle properties of parallelograms will be introduced in this section.

1. The opposite angles of a parallelogram are equal.

2. Each pair of angles between two parallel sides adds up to 180°.

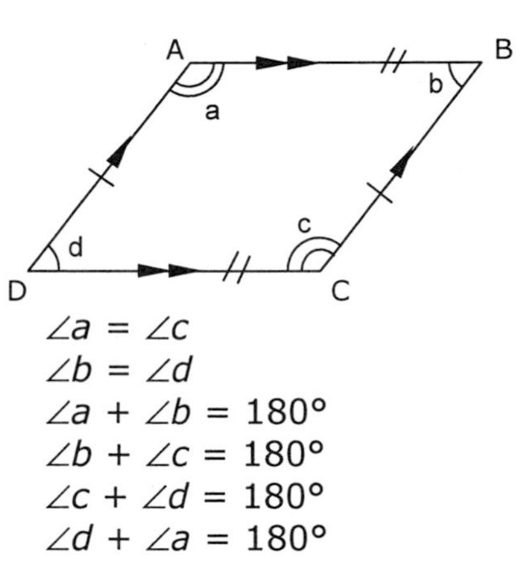

Since rectangles, rhombuses, and squares are also parallelograms, these properties apply to them as well.

Trapezoids have one set of parallel sides, so the pair of angles between them adds up to 180°.

In drawings, an equal number of markings indicate equal lines (marked by short perpendicular lines), parallel lines (marked by arrows going in the same direction), or equal angles (marked by arcs). In the diagram above, the markings indicate that AB = DC, DA = CB, AB // DC, AD // BC, $\angle a = \angle c$, and $\angle b = \angle d$.

In solving for unknown angles, do not require students to write down the reasons for each calculation, but they should be able to justify their steps in oral discussion.

Students have learned that the sum of the angles of a triangle is 180°. You may want to teach them that the sum of the angles of a 4-sided figure is 360°. This will be useful if you want to show them why all quadrilaterals tessellate in the next unit. Any quadrilateral (4-sided figure) can be divided into two triangles. The sum of the angles of these two triangles together is the same as the sum of the angles of the quadrilateral. In the figure shown here:

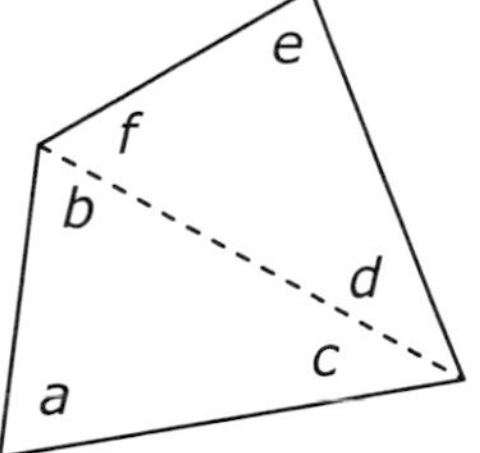

$$\begin{aligned}\text{Sum of the angles} &= (\angle a + \angle b + \angle c) + (\angle d + \angle e + \angle f)\\ &= 180^\circ + 180^\circ\\ &= 360^\circ.\end{aligned}$$

In general, a polygon of n sides can be divided up into $n - 2$ triangles, so the sum of the angles is $180^\circ \times (n - 2)$. If the polygon is a regular polygon (equilateral and equiangular) then the measure of each angle is $\frac{180^\circ \times (n-2)}{n}$

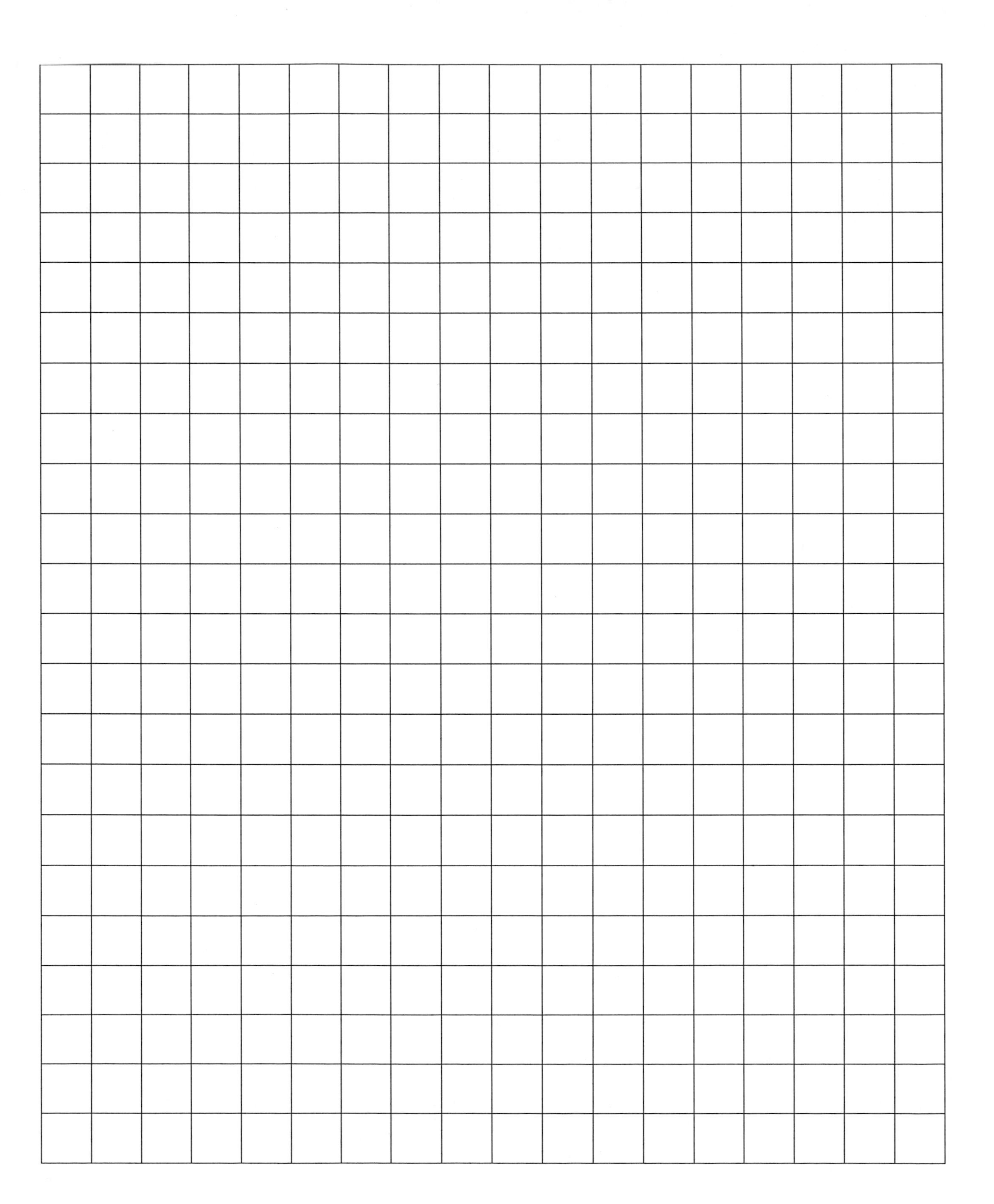

Activity 7.1a **4-sided figures**

1. Review properties of rectangles.
   - Draw a rectangle on the board, write *rectangle* under it. Ask student to tell you what they know about rectangles.
   - Lead them to say (and write on the board):
     - The corners of a rectangle are right angles (90°).
     - The perimeter of a rectangle is 2 times the length plus 2 times the width.
     - The area of a rectangle is the length times the width.
   - Emphasize (and write on the board):
     - The opposite sides of the rectangle are parallel to each other.
     - The adjacent sides of the rectangle are perpendicular to each other.

2. Introduce parallelograms.
   - Tell students that now we will learn about other kinds of 4-sided figures.
   - Tell students that a rectangle is a special case of 4-sided figures called *parallelograms.* A parallelogram is any 4-sided figure constructed with two pairs of parallel lines.
   - Draw a parallelogram on the board. Tell them that a 4-sided figure constructed with two pairs of parallel lines is a parallelogram. And, unlike the rectangle, a parallelogram's corners do not have to be right angles.
   - Write the word *Parallelogram* on the board.
   - Refer to **p. 68 in the textbook**. Have students find those figures with two pairs of parallel lines (A, B, D, and E) and copy them onto centimeter graph paper.
   - Emphasize that each of these 4-sided figures (A, B, D and E) has two pairs of parallel sides, and that these figures are all called *parallelograms*.
   - Have them mark one pair of their sides with a single arrow and the other pair with a double arrow. Tell students that these marks indicate which sides are parallel to each other. Have students write the word *parallelogram* in or next to their drawn figures.

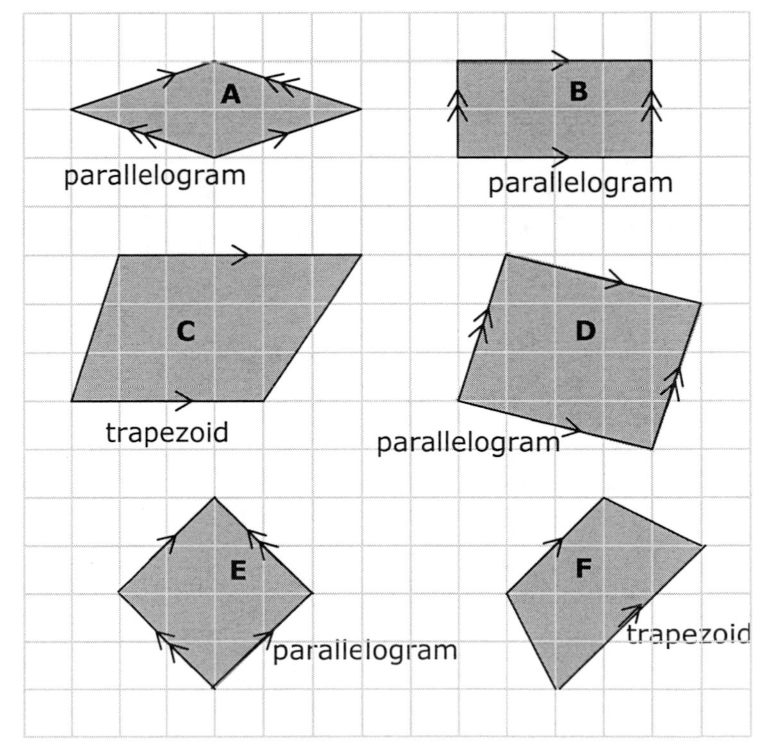

3. Introduce trapezoids.
   - Again, refer to **p. 68 in the textbook**. Have students find the figures with only one pair of parallel lines (C and F) and copy these figures onto centimeter graph paper.
   - Have them mark the parallel lines with a single arrow.
   - Draw a trapezoid on the board. Tell students that any 4-sided figure with one pair (but not two pairs) of parallel sides is called a *trapezoid* [trapeziums for 3rd edition].
   - Write the word on the board and have them write the word in or next to their drawn figures.

4. Introduce rhombuses.
   - Now have students determine which sides are equal for all the figures (A, B, C, D, E, F), and mark their equal sides (one-cross hair for one pair of equal sides, and two for a second pair.
   - Point out that parallelograms B, D and E each has two pairs of equal sides. Parallelograms A and E also have two pairs of equal sides, but have all sides equal.
   - Point out that for the two trapezoids, F has two equal sides, but C has no equal sides. They should note that trapezoids may or may not have any equal sides; but if they do, it is not their parallel sides which are equal. (If a figure's parallel sides are equal, it is a parallelogram; not a trapezoid.)
   - Tell students a parallelogram that has all 4 sides equal is called a *rhombus*. Write the word on the board and have them write the word in or next to figures A and E.

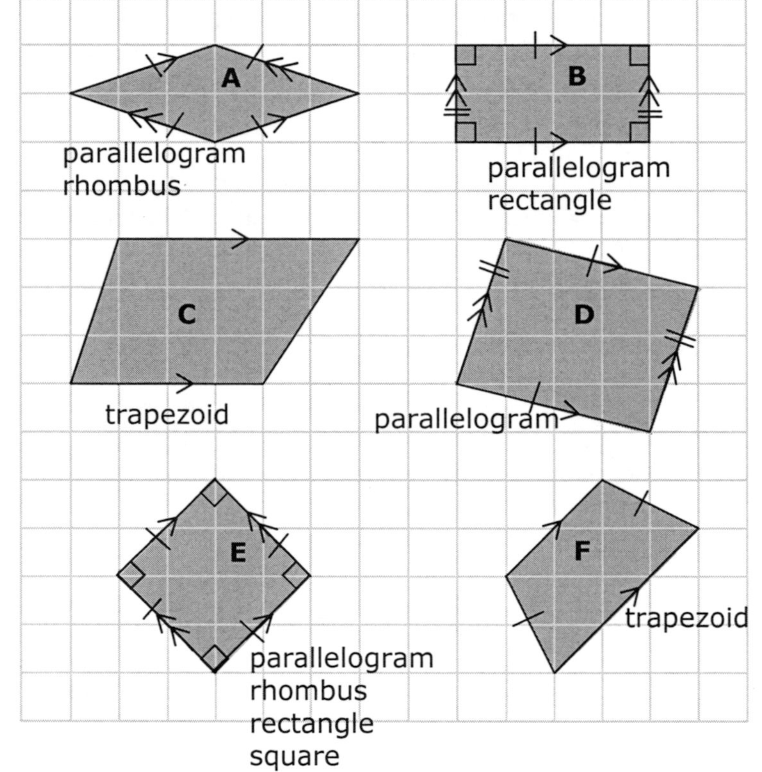

5. Relate rectangles and squares to parallelograms and rhombuses.
   - Have students mark right angles with little squares. Tell students that parallelograms with 4 right angles are called rectangles. Have them label B and E as rectangles.
   - Ask them to compare figures B and E. E has four equal sides. Ask students what this figure is called. It is a square. Have them label E as a square. They should notice that a square is a rectangle, a rhombus, and a parallelogram.

6. Review
   - Make sure students understand that there are two main types of figures here – parallelograms and trapezoids.
     - Parallelograms have two pairs of parallel sides; trapezoids have only one pair of parallel sides
     - Rhombuses are a special kind of parallelogram with 4 equal sides.
     - Rectangles are a special kind of parallelogram with 4 right angles.
     - Squares are a special kind of rectangle with 4 equal sides, and a special kind of rhombus with 4 right angles.
   - Provide students with 4 straws and pins, or geostrips of 2 different lengths and fasteners. Have them form a rectangle by fastening the geostrips or by putting a pin through both straws at the corner.
   - Have the students move their geostrips or straws to change the rectangle into a parallelogram. They should see that the opposite sides remain equal and parallel, even though the angles are no longer right angles.
   - They can repeat this with straws of the same lengths for a square and a rhombus.

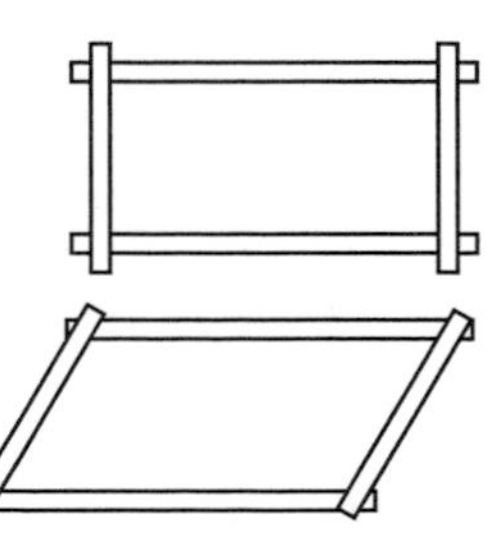

Activity 7.1b **Angle properties of parallelograms**

1. Investigate angle properties of parallelograms.
   - Have students do **tasks 1-2, textbook pp. 69-70**. Rather than having students trace and cut out the parallelogram, you can provide them with square graph paper and have them draw a variety of parallelograms.
   - Students should label each corner on both sides of the cut-out shapes to keep track of them.
   - In task 1, one part is flipped both horizontally and vertically to match up opposite corners. In task 2, one part is slid either down or over to line up the angles.
   - Have students use the square graph paper to draw and cut out a rhombus, or provide them with paper rhombuses.
     - Ask them to fold it in half. They can see that the sides are equal. Ask them what shape is formed. It is an isosceles triangle.
     - Have them fold it in half again to see that all 4 sides are equal. Then have them unfold it. The crease shows that a line from one corner to the opposite corner divides the rhombus into isosceles triangles.

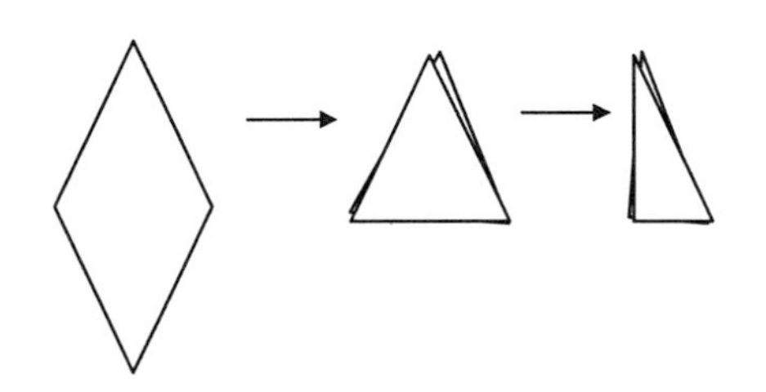

2. Find unknown angles in parallelograms.
   - Have students do **tasks 3-4, textbook pp. 70-71**. Note that in task 4, $\angle z$ is a base angle of an isosceles triangle.

Workbook Exercises 45-46

In these exercises, students should not assume that adjacent sides (sides that are not opposite to each other) are equal, even though they look equal in the drawing; unless they are told they are equal or told that the figure is a rhombus.

Possible solutions:

Exercise 45

(a)	$\angle a = 55°$	Opposite $\angle$s of a parallelogram are equal
(b)	$\angle b = 180° - 75° = 105°$	Sum of pairs of $\angle$s between two // lines = 180°
(c)	$\angle c = 125°$	Opposite $\angle$s of a parallelogram are equal
(d)	$\angle d + 18° + 142° = 180°$ $\angle d = 180° - 18° - 142° = 20°$	Sum of pairs of $\angle$s between two // lines = 180°
(e)	$\angle e = 110°$	Opposite $\angle$s of a parallelogram are equal
(f)	$\angle f + 60° + 60° = 180°$ $\angle f = 180° - 60° - 60° = 60°$	Sum of pairs of $\angle$s between two // lines = 180°
(g)	$\angle g = 180° - 80° = 100°$	Sum of pairs of $\angle$s between two // lines =180°
(h)	$\angle h = 135°$	Opposite $\angle$s of a parallelogram are equal.

Exercise 46

(a) $\angle a = 100°$	Opposite $\angle$s of a parallelogram (a rhombus is a parallelogram) are equal.
(b) $\angle b = 180° - (2 \times 75°) = 30°$	Half of a rhombus is an isosceles triangle.
(c) $\angle c = 56°$	Opposite $\angle$s of a rhombus are equal.
(d) $\angle d + 73° = 180°$ $\angle d = 180° - 73° = 107°$	Sum of pairs of $\angle$s between two // lines = 180°
(e) $\angle e + 40° = 180°$ $\angle e = 180° - 40° = 140°$	Sum of pairs of $\angle$s between two // lines = 180°
(f) $\angle f + 135° = 180°$ $\angle f = 180° - 135° = 45°$	Sum of pairs of $\angle$s between two // lines = 180°
(g) $\angle g = 180° - (2 \times 60°) = 60°$	Half of a rhombus is an isosceles triangle.
(h) $\angle h + 50° + 80° = 180°$ $\angle h = 180° - 50° - 80° = 50°$	Sum of pairs of $\angle$s between two // lines = 180°
Alternate solution: $\angle h = 50°$	The bisector (line between opposite angles) is a line of symmetry.

Activity 7.1c **Find unknown angles**

1. Investigate angle properties of parallelograms.
   - Have students use square graph paper to draw and cut out some trapezoids. Then, have them cut the trapezoids between the parallel sides so that they can slide the pieces to see that the sum of angles between the two parallel sides is 180° (they make a straight line).
   - Each pair of angles between two parallel sides adds up to 180°.
   - Tell students that the converse is also true: If the angles between two sides add up to 180°, then the sides are parallel.

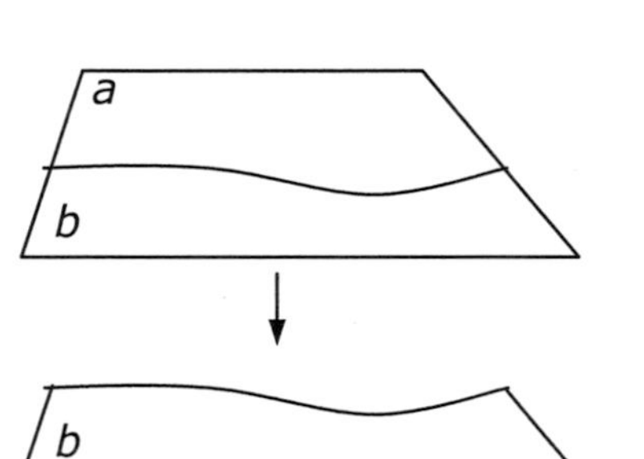

2. Discuss **task 5, textbook p. 71**.

3. Have students do **task 6, textbook p. 71**.
   - Note that each solution is found by knowing that the sum of pairs of $\angle$s between two // lines =180°.
   - The solution for $\angle c$ also requires knowing that:
     The $\angle$ next to 22° angle = 50°, because the larger triangle is isosceles.
     So, $\angle c = 180° - (22° + 50°) = 108°$, since the sum of pairs of angles between two parallel lines is 180°.

4. (Optional) Explore shapes.
   - Provide students with copies of the next page of this guide. Have them cut them out, or provide them with the shapes already cut out.
   - Have students see if they can do the following:
     - ➢ Cut the parallelogram into two pieces that can be rearranged to form a rectangle.

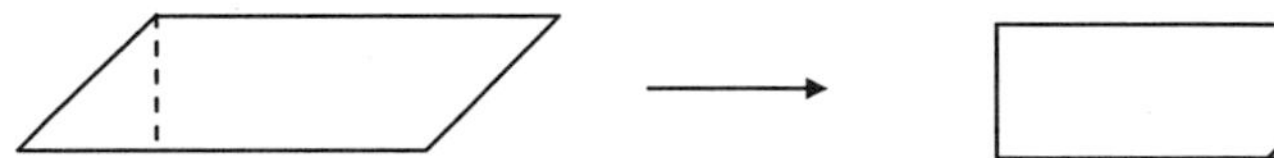

     - ➢ Cut a rectangle into two triangles that can be rearranged to form a parallelogram.
     - ➢ Cut a trapezoid into two pieces that can be rearranged to form a parallelogram.

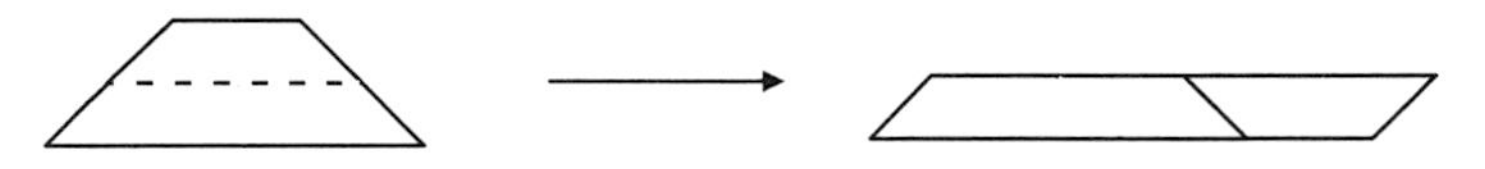

Workbook Exercise 47

(a) $\angle a = 180° - 112° = 68°$ — Sum of pairs of $\angle$s between two // lines =180°

(b) $\angle b + 32° + 123° = 180°$ — Sum of pairs of $\angle$s between two // lines =180°
$\angle b = 180° - 32° - 123° = 25°$

(c) $\angle c = 180° - 84° = 96°$ — Sum of pairs of $\angle$s between two // lines =180°
$\angle x = 180° - 48° = 132°$ — Sum of pairs of $\angle$s between two // lines =180°

(d) $\angle d = 25° + 87° = 112°$ — Exterior angle equal to opposite interior angles
$\angle y = 180° - 112° = 68°$ — Sum of pairs of $\angle$s between two // lines =180°
Alternative solution:
$\angle$ adjacent to $\angle d$
$= 180° - 87° - 25° = 68°$ — Sum of $\angle$s of a triangle = 180°
$\angle d = 180° - 68° = 112°$ — Sum of adjacent $\angle$s on a straight line = 180°
$\angle y = 180° - d = 180° - 112° = 68°$ — Sum of pairs of $\angle$s between two // lines =180°

(e) $\angle e = 180° - 100° = 80°$ — Sum of pairs of $\angle$s between two // lines =180°

(f) $\angle f = 180° - 84° - 78° = 18°$ — Sum of pairs of $\angle$s between two // lines =180°

(g) $\angle g = 180° - 132° = 48°$ — Sum of pairs of $\angle$s between two // lines =180°
$\angle$ adjacent to z = $180° - 59° = 121°$ — Sum of pairs of $\angle$s between two // lines =180°
$\angle z = 180° - 121° = 59°$ — Adjacent $\angle$s on a straight line

(h)

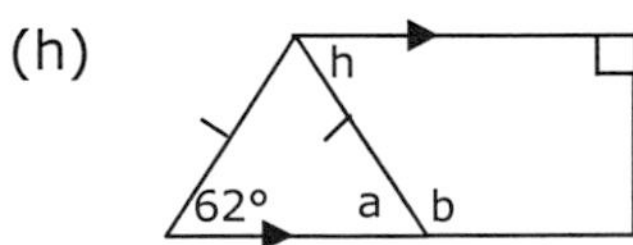

$\angle a = 62°$ — isosceles triangle
$\angle b = 180 - 62° = 118°$ — adjacent $\angle$s on a straight line
$\angle h = 180° - 118° =$ **62°** — pair of $\angle$s between two // lines

---

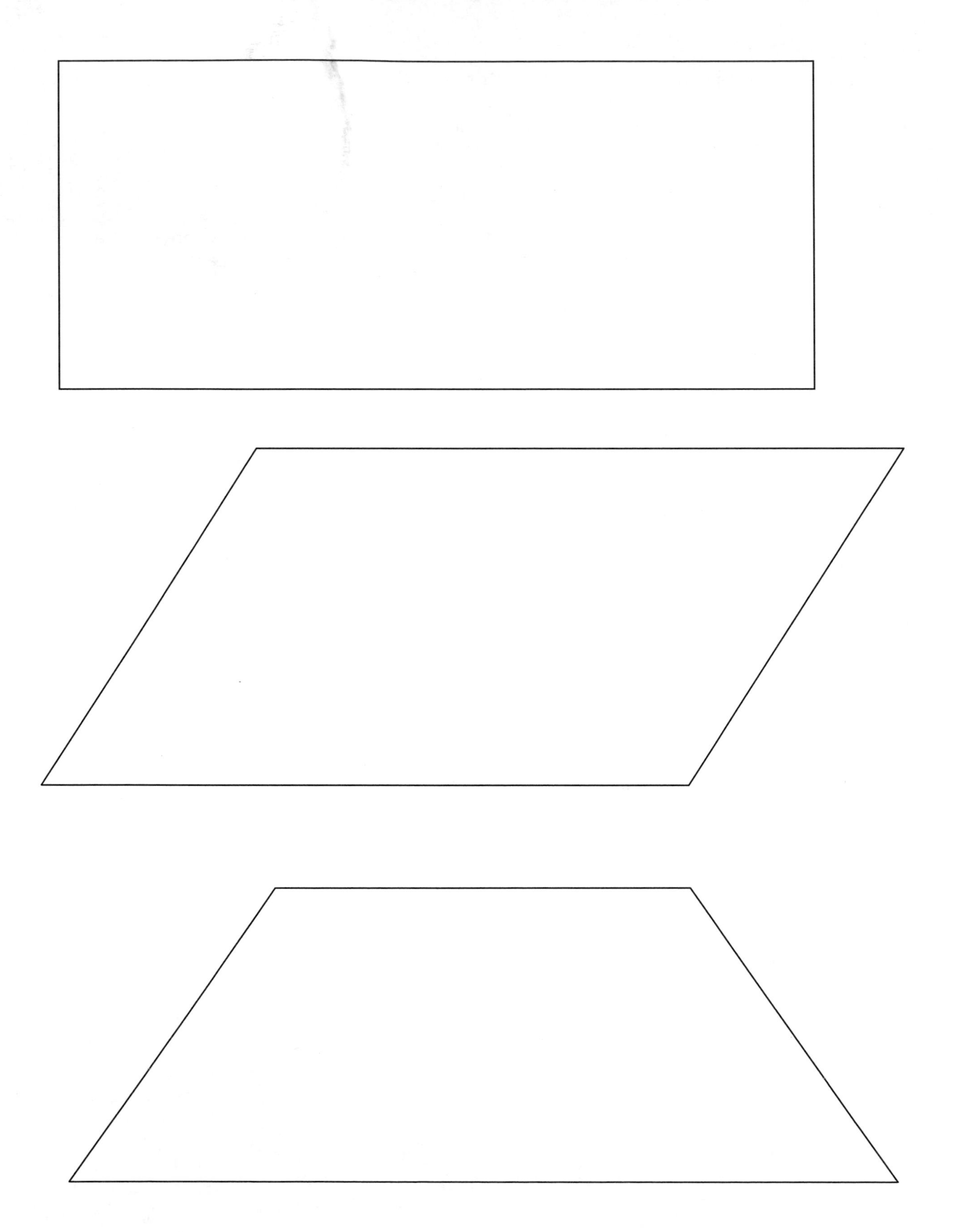

Part 2: Drawing Parallelograms and Rhombuses — 2 sessions

Objectives

- Construct a parallelogram.
- Construct a rectangle with a given length and width.
- Construct a parallelogram when given the measurement of two adjacent sides and one angle.
- Construct a rhombus when given the measurement of one side and one angle.

Materials

- Protractors
- Rulers
- Set-squares

Homework

- Workbook Exercise 48

Notes

In this section, students will learn to draw parallelograms and rhombuses from given measurements of sides and angles. If a sketch isn't provided in the problem, students should make a sketch of the figure before drawing it full scale.

Although parallelograms and rhombuses can be drawn using compasses, students will not be learning those techniques here.

Activity 7.2a **Drawing rectangles and parallelograms**

1. Draw parallelograms.
   - Refer to **textbook p. 72**. Guide students in drawing a parallelogram.
   - Have students practice drawing perpendicular lines, parallel lines, and parallelograms using a set-square and ruler.

2. Draw rectangles.
   - Refer to **task 1, textbook p. 73**. Guide students in following the directions for drawing the rectangle.
   - Then, have students draw rectangles with given measurements. For example:
     - ➢ Draw a rectangle ABCD in which AB = 10 cm and BC = 2 cm.
     - ➢ Draw a rectangle with length 5 inches and width 4 inches.
     - ➢ Draw a square with side 5 cm.

3. Draw parallelograms.
   - Refer to **task 2, textbook p. 74**. Guide students in following directions for drawing the parallelogram.
   - Have students do **task 3, textbook p. 75**.

Workbook Exercise 48, problems 1 and 2

Activity 7.2b **Drawing parallelograms and rhombuses**

1. Draw rhombuses.
   Refer to **task 4, textbook p. 75**. Guide students in drawing a rhombus.
   Have students do **task 5, textbook p. 75**.

2. Give students the measurements (two the sides and one angle) of some parallelograms to draw. Have students first draw a small sketch of the figure, estimating the angles, and then construct a full-scale drawing. You can also have them draw a trapezoid. For example:
   - ➢ Draw a parallelogram ABCD in which AB = 7 cm, AD = 3 cm, $\angle$ABC = 100°. Measure $\angle$BCD. (80°)
   - ➢ Draw a rhombus WXYZ in which WX = 6 cm, and $\angle$ZWX = 25°. Measure $\angle$WXY. (155°)
   - ➢ Draw a trapezoid PQRS where PQ = 9 cm, PS = 5 cm, $\angle$SPQ = 60°, and $\angle$PQR = 90°.

Workbook Exercise 48, problems 3 and 4

Unit 8 – Tessellations

Objectives

- Identify the shape used in tessellations.
- Draw tessellations on dot paper.
- Determine whether a shape can tessellate.
- Make different tessellations with a given shape.

Suggested number of sessions: 4

	Objectives	Textbook	Workbook	Activities
Part 1 : Tiling Patterns				**4 sessions**
59	▪ Understand tessellation. ▪ Identify the shape used in a tessellation. ▪ Draw a tessellation on dot paper.	p. 76 p. 77, task 1	Ex. 49	8.1a
60	▪ Determine whether a shape can tessellate. ▪ Explore properties of shapes that can tessellate.	P 78, task 2	Ex. 50	8.1b
61	▪ Make different tessellations with a given shape.	p. 79, tasks 3-4	Ex. 51-52	8.1c
62	▪ Make shapes that can tessellate.		Review 2	8.1d

Part 1: Tiling Patterns — 4 sessions

Objectives

- Identify the shape used in a tessellation.
- Continue a tessellation on dot paper.
- Determine whether a shape can tessellate or not.
- Make different tessellations with a given shape.

Materials

- Cardboard or paper shapes
- Square and isometric dot paper
- Examples of tessellations such as fabrics, gift wrapping paper, art by M.C. Escher
- Blank transparencies, dry-erase markers

Homework

- Workbook Exercise 49
- Workbook Exercise 50
- Workbook Exercise 51
- Workbook Exercise 52

Notes

A tessellation is an arrangement of congruent shapes on a flat surface. They are geometric patterns that are made of one or more shapes that are fitted together to make a repeating pattern. This ancient form of decoration dates back to the 4th century B.C. A pattern is a tessellation if:

1. It is made of one or more shapes that can be extended in every direction to cover a surface, and
2. The pattern pieces fit together without any gaps or overlapping.

This unit will deal only with tessellations that are made with a single shape.

Students will be using some given shapes to see if they can tessellate. It is not necessary for them to come up with a generalization about which shapes can tessellate or not.

For your information, there are only 3 regular polygons (polygons with equal sides and angles) that will always form a tessellation using only one shape: a square, an equilateral triangle, and a regular hexagon. This is because their angles are a factor of 360°. Four square angles will make a complete rotation around a point. The angles of a hexagon are 120°, so three hexagons can make a complete rotation.

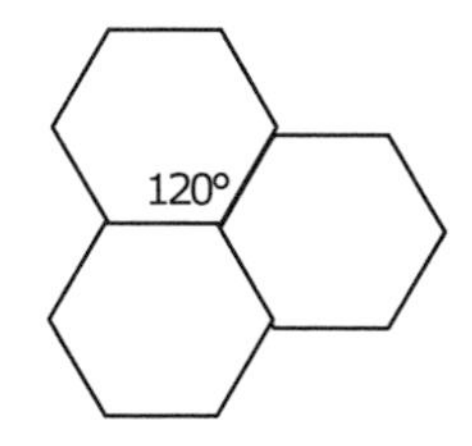

Rectangles will also tessellate, in a number of different ways. They can also be combined to form a variety of shapes that will tessellate.

A parallelogram will tessellate by translation.

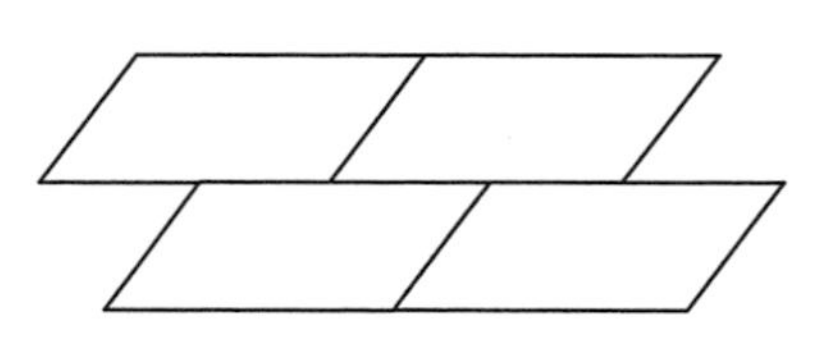

Cutting a parallelogram from one corner to the opposite corner gives two triangles which are the same, so a triangle will tessellate.

Trapezoids will tessellate because two of them make a parallelogram.

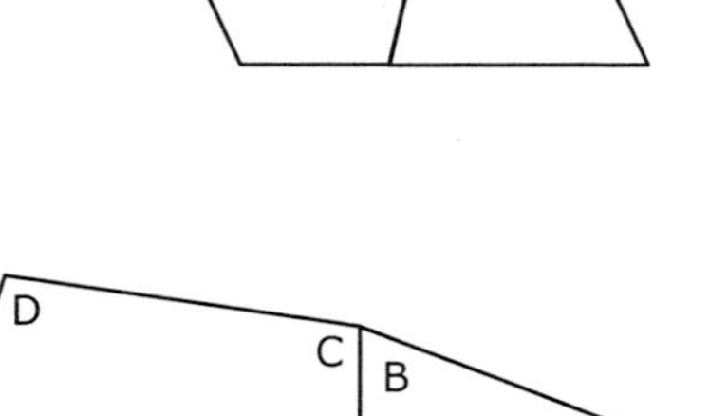

A general quadrilateral will tessellate by having all 4 different corners meet at a point, since the sum of the angles of a quadrilateral is 360°, and the sides will match up in length.

All triangles will tessellate, since the sum of their angles is 180°. The triangle can be copied and rotated so that one side fits against the same side of the original, forming a quadrilateral. The resulting quadrilateral will tessellate.

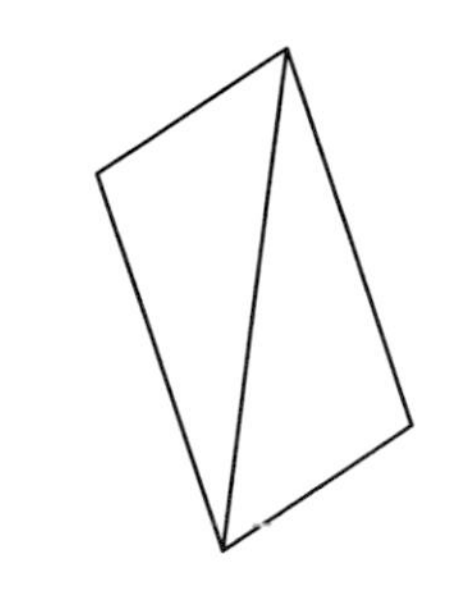

Many other figures can tessellate. The last activity for this unit (8.1d) shows how some figures which tessellate can be constructed from other figures which are known to tessellate.

Activity 8.1a **Tessellations**

1. Look for repeating shapes in tessellations.
   - Discuss **p. 76 in the textbook**. Students should notice that the shape repeats, that there are no gaps in the repeating design, and that the shape can be added to extend the design in any direction.
   - Tell students that a pattern formed by fitting pieces of the same shape together without any gaps or overlaps is called a *tessellation*.
   - Have students do **task 1, textbook p. 77**. You can give students clear transparency sheets or other plastic sheets, such as page protectors, which they can lay over these tessellations. They can trace the shape with a marker and move the sheet around to see that the same shape is used repeatedly in each tessellation. The shape may be rotated.
   - Have students identify tessellations in the environment such as tiled floors, designs on fabric and gift wrapping, and some art work. Tessellations can have more than one shape; as long as there are no gaps in the design, the shapes repeat, and the design can be extended in any direction.
   - You can ask students to look around at home to see if they see any examples of tessellations. They can sketch what they see, or bring in a sample.

2. Create tessellations from given shapes.
   - Provide students with some dot paper and shapes that can tessellate. Get them to draw the tessellations on dot paper by moving the shapes around and tracing. The dot paper is just to help them orient the figure, and students can use the dots to help draw the figures. You can use the figures on the next page.
   - Students could also work in groups. Provide each group with 20 of the same shape and have them arrange these into a tessellation, and then draw the result on dot paper. Some of the groups could be given the same shape so that students can see that there can be different ways to tessellate one shape.

Workbook Exercise 49

Activity 8.1b **Tessellations**

1. Determine whether a shape can tessellate.
   - Discuss the first part of **task 2, textbook p. 78**. Not all shapes can tessellate.
   - Have students do the second part of this task. You can copy p. 102 of this guide and use the square dot paper rather than having them trace the figures in the book. Instead of making 12 copies, students could just use one copy, trace it onto the dot paper, and move it to trace it again.
   - Provide students with some additional shapes, some of which can tessellate and some of which cannot. Ask them to determine which ones cannot tessellate.
   - You may want to discuss why quadrilaterals and triangles can always tessellate.

Workbook Exercise 50

Shapes that can tessellate

Shapes that cannot tessellate

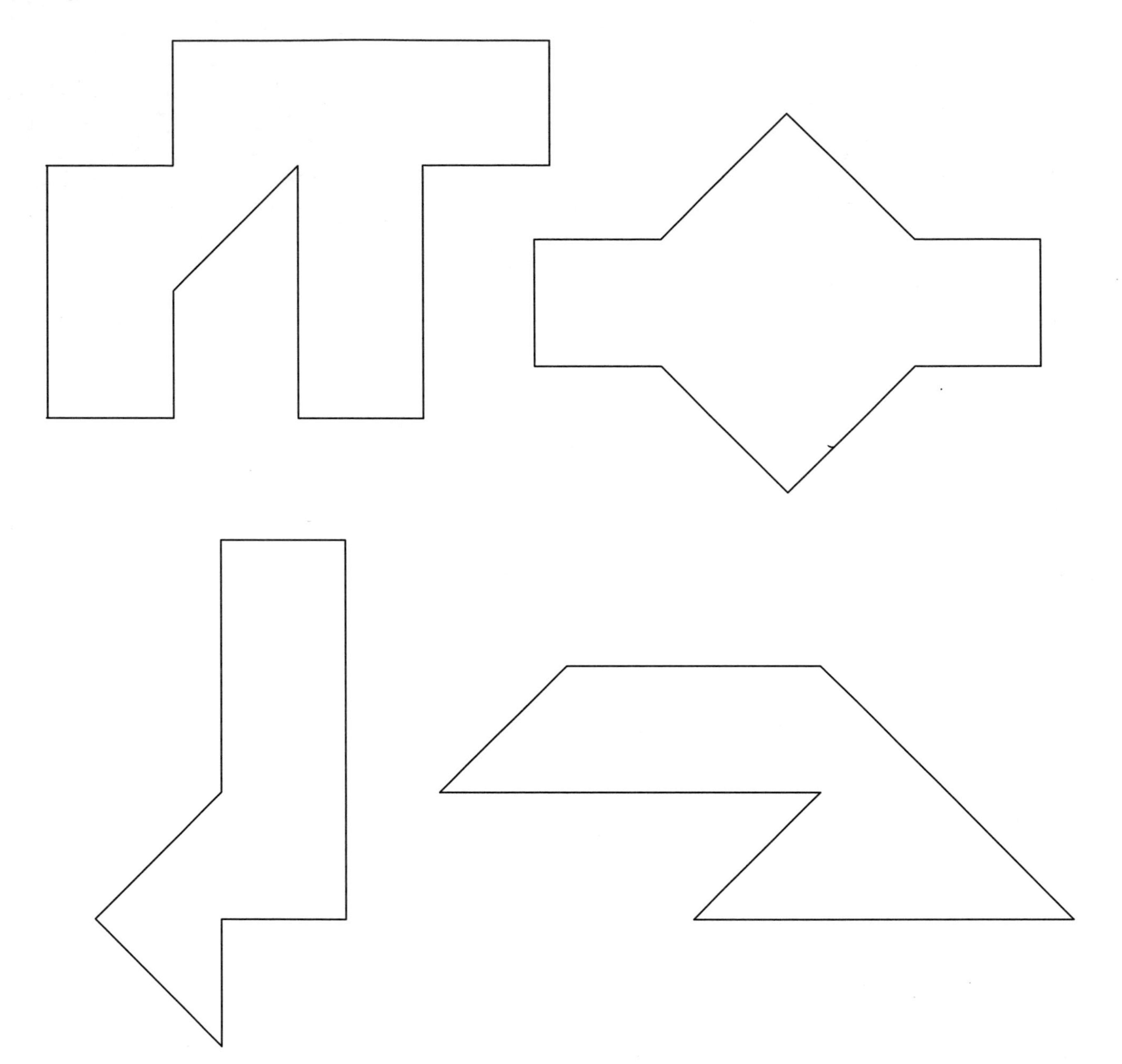

Figures from pp. 78 and 79 in the textbook

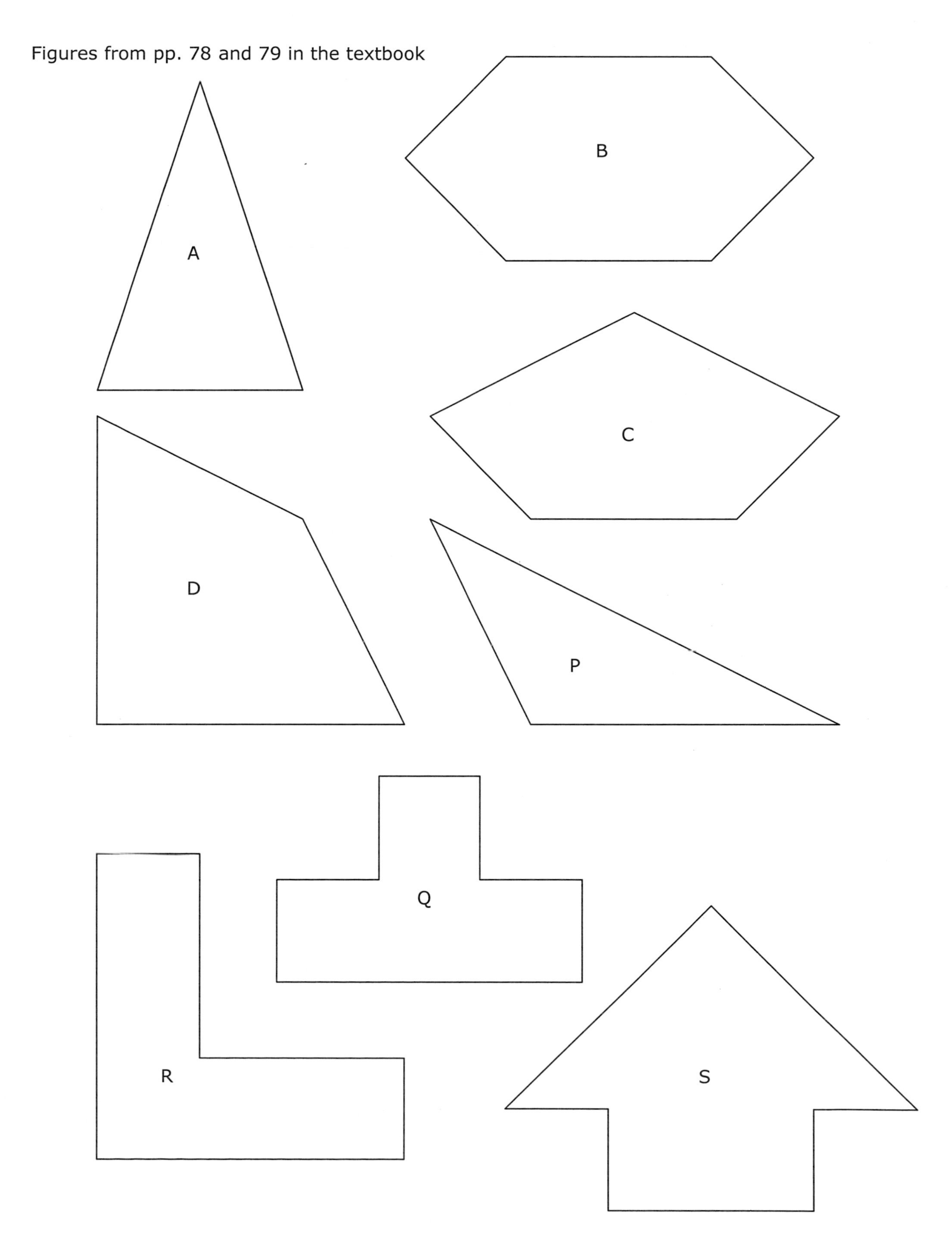

Activity 8.1c **Tessellations**

1. Make different tessellations with a given shape.
   - Discuss **task 3, textbook p. 79**.
   - Provide students with square dot paper and a rectangle shape and have them see how many tessellations they can make with the rectangle.
   - Have students do **task 4, textbook p. 79**. You can copy the previous page of this guide and use the square dot paper instead of having them trace the figures in the book.

Workbook Exercises 51-52

Activity 8.1d (optional) **Design shapes that can tessellate**

M.C. Escher is a famous artist who created a wide variety of shapes that can tessellate. Many of his creations are things in nature like fish, birds, insects, and dinosaurs. If students are interested, you can show them the following methods for creating Escher-types of shapes. Once a tessellating shape is created they can trace it, cut it out, and copy it to make the tessellation. They can also add features to the design.

You can modify a rectangle by cutting one side and sliding it over to the other side.

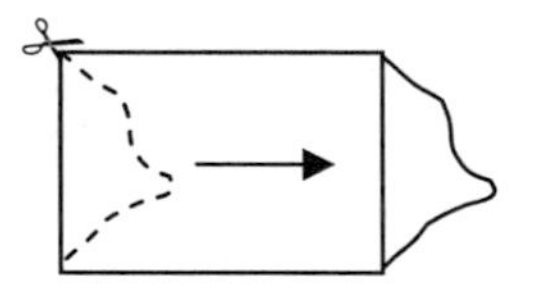

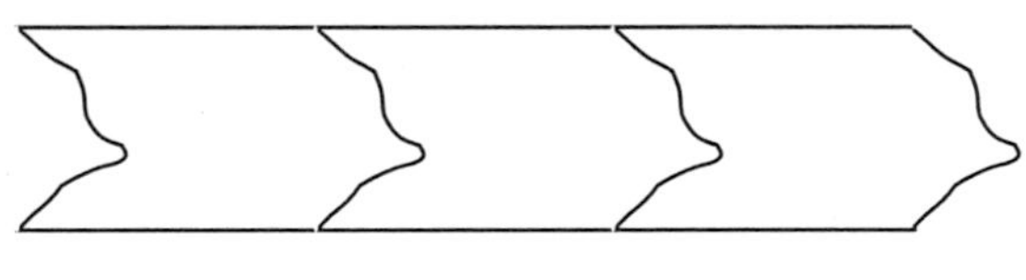

You can also modify the other side.

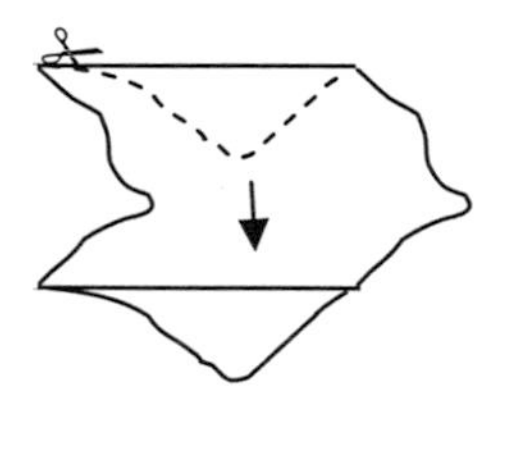

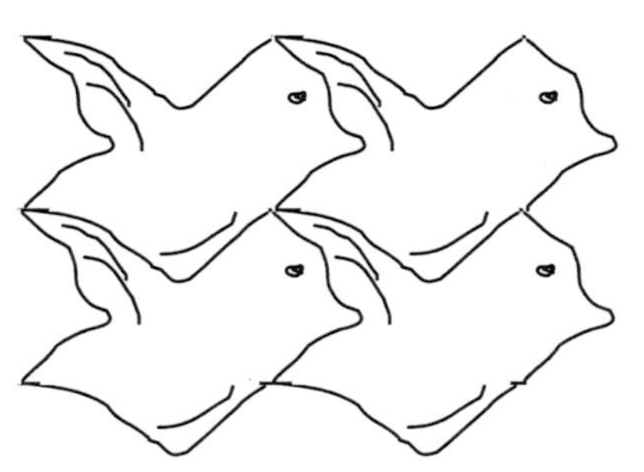

Tessellations can be created from triangles by marking the midpoint on each side, cutting a piece from one half of one side, and rotating it 180° around the midpoint. You can do this with each side.

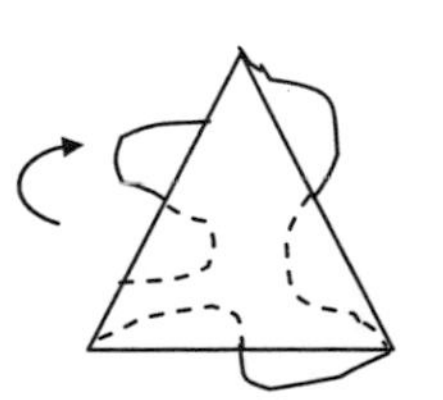

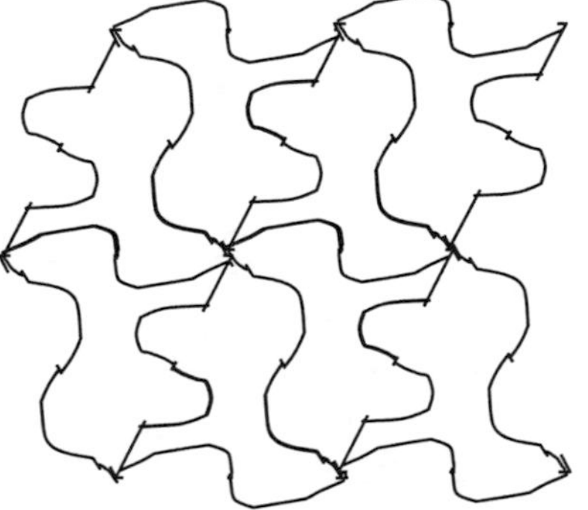

Workbook Review 2

Unit 9 – Volume

Objectives

- Find the side of a cuboid when given its volume and either the dimension of the other two sides or the area of one face.
- Find the volume of a solid by the volume of the liquid displaced.
- Solve word problems involving volume and liquid displaced by solids.

Suggested number of sessions: 6

	Objectives	Textbook	Workbook	Activities
Part 1 : Cubes and Cuboids				**3 sessions**
63	▪ Find the volume of solids made from unit cubes. ▪ Find the side of a cube when given its volume. ▪ Find one dimension of a cuboid if given its volume and the other two dimensions, or the area of a face.	p. 80 pp. 81, tasks 1-3 p. 83, task 5	Ex. 53, #1-2	9.1a
64	▪ Review the equivalency of 1 liter with 1000 cm^3. ▪ Find the height of water in rectangular-based containers when given the volume of water in liters and the length and width of the base.	P 82, task 4	Ex. 53 #3-4	9.1b
65	▪ Solve word problems of up to 2-steps involving volume.	p. 82, task 6	Ex. 54	9.1c
Part 2 : Finding the Volume of a Solid				**3 sessions**
66	▪ Recognize that the volume of the liquid displaced by a solid is equal to the volume of the solid.	p. 83		9.2a
67	▪ Solve word problems of up to 2-steps involving displacement of liquid by a solid.	p. 84, tasks 1-2	Ex. 55	9.2b
68	▪ Practice.	p. 85, Practice 9A		9.2c

Part 1: Cubes and Cuboids — 3 sessions

Objectives

- Find the length of the side of a cube when given its volume.
- Find one dimension of a cuboid when given its volume and the other two dimensions.
- Find one dimension of a cuboid when given its volume and the area of one face.
- Solve word problems of up to 2-steps involving the volume of cuboids or cubes and the volume of liquids.

Materials

- Connect-a-cubes or multilink cubes, about 65 for each group of students
- Base-10 blocks (unit cube and 1000 cube)
- 100 ml graduated cylinder or beaker

Homework

- Workbook Exercise 53
- Workbook Exercise 54

Notes

A cuboid is a rectangular parallelepiped, i.e. a "box" shape.

In *Primary Mathematics 4B*, students learned to find the volume of a cuboid when given its length, width, and height, and of a cube when given one side. This is reviewed here.

$$\text{volume} = \text{length} \times \text{width} \times \text{height}$$

If the volume and two of the other dimensions of a cuboid are known, we can find the third dimension by dividing the volume by the two known dimensions. For example, if we are given the length and width, the height can be found by dividing the volume by the length and width.

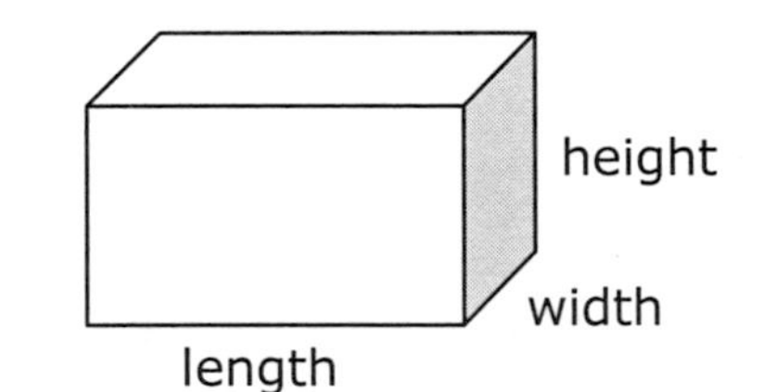

$$\text{height} = \frac{\text{volume}}{\text{length} \times \text{width}}$$

For a cube, since all three dimensions are the same, we can find the length of the side of a cube from its volume. At this level, all volumes given for cubes will be perfect cubes. For example, a cube with a volume of 27 cm^3 has sides of 3 cm, since $3 \times 3 \times 3 = 27$. Students should memorize the perfect cubes to 1000, or at least through 125 and be able to find the others as needed. So, for example, if they are given a volume of 343 cm^3 for a cube, they should realize that the side must be larger than 5 (since $5 \times 5 \times 5 = 125$), and that the side can't be 6, since $6 \times 6 \times 6$ gives an even number; so they can try $7 \times 7 \times 7$.

s	s^3
1	1
2	8
3	27
4	64
5	125
6	216
7	343
8	512
9	729
10	1000

If we are given the area of one of the faces of the cuboid, we can find the third dimension. The area is the other two dimensions multiplied together.

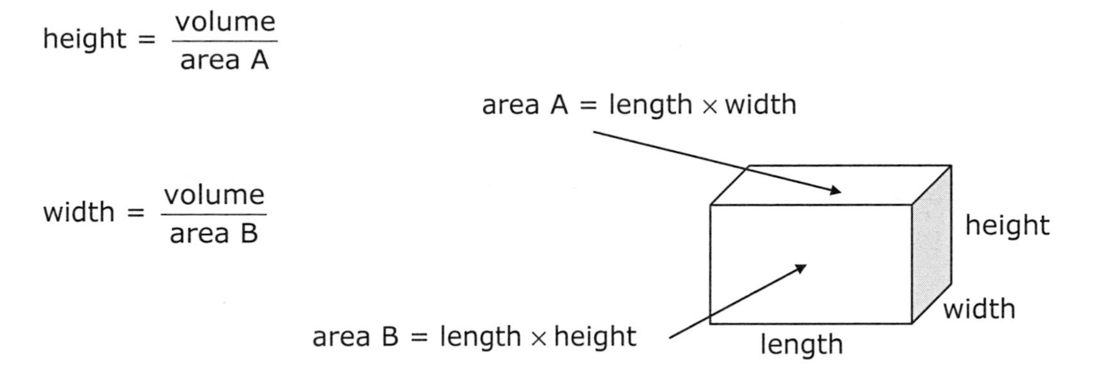

Students also learned in *Primary Mathematics 4B* that 1 cm^3 is the same as 1 milliliter and 1000 cm^3 is the same as 1 liter. They could then solve volume problems involving water in a container shaped like a cuboid. The problems in this section will generally involve the addition or removal of liquids. Given the volume of the liquid that is added or removed, and two of the dimensions (length and width), we can divide the volume of water by the length and by the width to find the change in height.

For example, if the plastic box shown here contains 1.5 liters of water, we can find the height of the water level as follows:

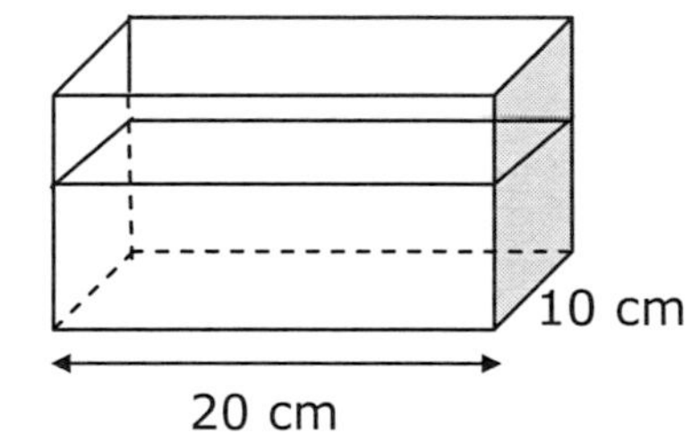

$1.5\ \ell = 1500\text{ cm}^3$

Height of water level $= \frac{1500}{20 \times 10} = 7.5$ cm

Activity 9.1a **Volume**

1. Review the volume of cuboids.
   - Divide students into groups and provide each group with 60 connect-a-cubes or multilink cubes.
     - o Ask each group to build a cuboid with the cubes.
     - o Remind them that a cuboid is a box shape. Each cuboid will not necessarily have the same shape, since one group could make a $4 \times 3 \times 5$ cuboid and another group might make a $6 \times 2 \times 5$ cuboid, for example.
     - o Ask them how they could find the volume of the cuboid, if they were only given the length, width, and height of the cuboid. Students will probably remember the formula: Volume = length $\times$ width $\times$ height. Point out that length $\times$ width gives the area of the bottom (and top) of the cuboid. If the cuboid had a height of 1 unit cube, i.e. just the bottom layer of cubes, then the volume would be length $\times$ width $\times$ 1 cubic units. When finding length $\times$ width $\times$ height, we are multiplying the area of the base by the number of layers of cubes.
   - Be sure that they realize that it is the cuboid's base, which is length $\times$ width, which is being multiplied by the height to find the volume. So if the cuboid has a height of 1 unit cube, it has one layer of cubes, and its volume in cubic units is length $\times$ width $\times$ 1. If it had 3 layers, its volume would be length $\times$ width $\times$ 3.
   - Illustrate this further by having them find the volume of a figure that is not a cuboid but one where they can find the area of the base.
     - o Ask students to use the cubes to make a 3 by 3 square connected to a 2 by 2 square and ask them to find the area.
     - o Then have them add 2 more layers and find the volume.
     - o Point out that we can find the volume by multiplying the area of the base by the height, as long as each layer is the same.

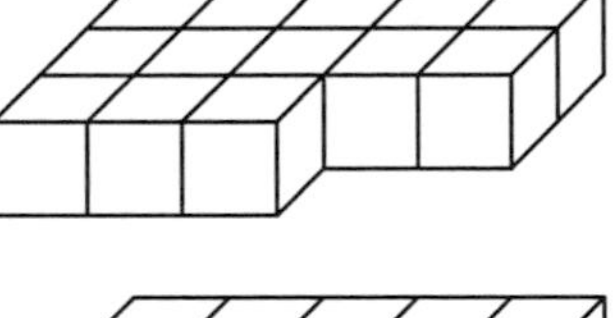

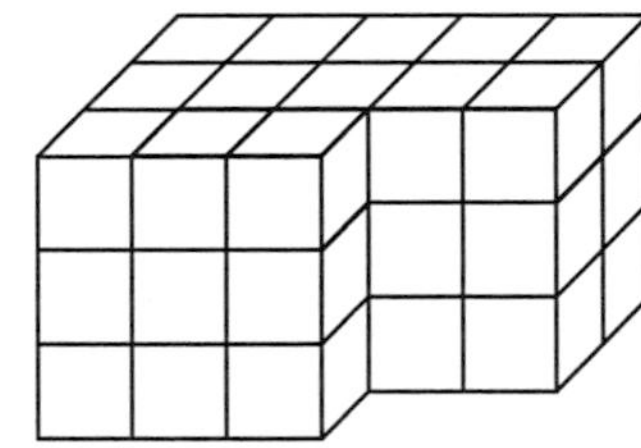

   - Discuss **p. 80 in the textbook**. Ask students to explain how they found the volumes of the solids. For A and D, they should split the figures up into cuboids rather than trying to count the blocks one by one. For example, the volume of D could be found as $(5 \times 2 \times 3) + (5 \times 2 \times 5)$ or $(5 \times 2 \times 2) + (5 \times 4 \times 3)$.

2. Find a dimension of a cuboid if given its volume, and the other two dimensions or the area of one face.
   - Ask them how they would build a cube using 64 cubes.
     - o Ask them what the length of the side would be.
     - o Then, ask students how we could find the length of the side without first building the cube. We would have to find some number for the side such that side $\times$ side $\times$ side = 64.
     - o Display a chart of the values of s $\times$ s $\times$ s for sides (s) from 1-10. These numbers are called perfect cubes. Tell students that if they know the perfect cubes, they can figure out how to build any cube.

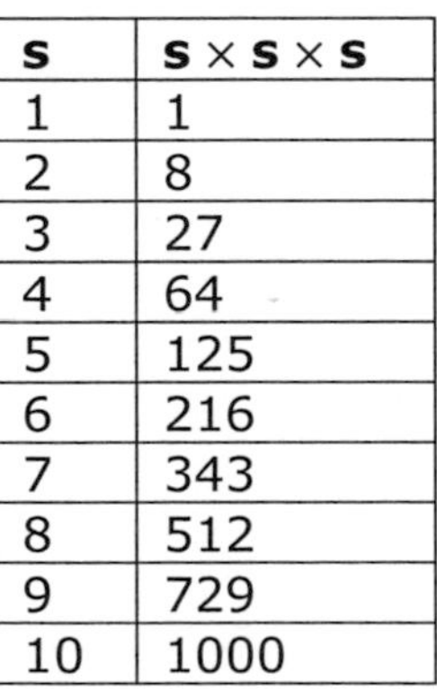

s	**s $\times$ s $\times$ s**
1	1
2	8
3	27
4	64
5	125
6	216
7	343
8	512
9	729
10	1000

- Divide students into groups and provide each group with connect-a-cubes. Ask them to build a cube with a volume of 27 cubic units, and then one with a volume of 8 cubic units.
- Now ask students to build a cuboid with a volume of 24 cubes, a length of 4 cubes, and a width of 3 cubes.
    - Then ask them to tell you the height. (2 cubes)
    - Ask them how we could find the height without building the cuboid. We have to divide the total volume by the number of cubes in one layer, which would be 3×4.
    - Ask them how we could find the width if they knew that the volume was 24, the height was 2, and the length was 4. This time, we would have to divide the total volume by the number of cubes in a different layer.
- Ask students to build a cuboid with a volume of 48 cubes and with area for the bottom of 16 square units.
    - Ask them for the height.
    - Ask students how we could find the height by calculations. We can divide the volume by the area of the base.

3. Discuss **tasks 1-3, textbook p. 81** and **task 5, textbook p. 82**.

Workbook Exercise 53, problems 1-2

Activity 9.1b **Liters and cubic centimeters**

1. Review conversion between milliliters and cubic centimeters.
    - Remind students that we use liters and milliliters for the volume of a liquid. We can also use cm^3.
    - Show students a centimeter cube. Tell them that if we made a waterproof box that just fit around this cube, its capacity would be exactly 1 milliliter. 1 milliliter of water fills the same amount of space as 1 cubic centimeter. A milliliter is about 20 drops of water.
    - Write the equation 1 ml = 1 cm^3 on the board.
    - Draw a box and label it in centimeters. Ask your students to find the volume in cubic centimeters and in milliliters.

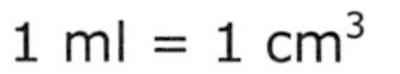

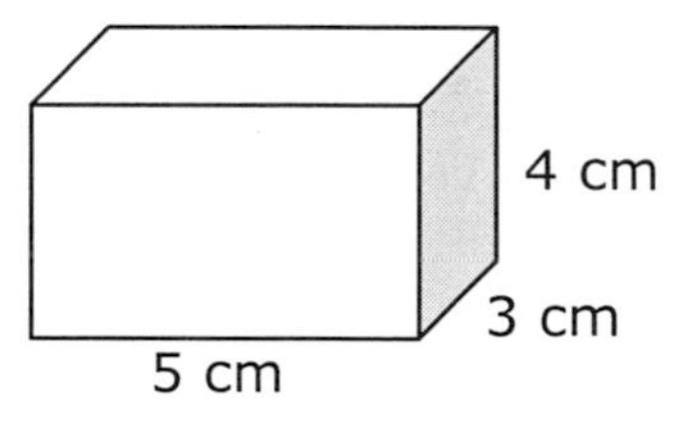

$$\text{Volume} = 5 \text{ cm} \times 3 \text{ cm} \times 4 \text{ cm} = 60 \text{ cm}^3 = 60 \text{ ml}$$

- Show students the thousand-cube from a base 10 set. Ask students how many unit cubes there are (1000). Each cube is a cubic centimeter. So if we had a container the same size as the thousand cube, it would hold 1000 cm^3, or 1000 ml of water. Since 1000 ml is 1 liter, and 1000 ml is 1000 cm^3, then 1 liter = 1000 cm^3. Show them the liter measuring cup and say the cube would hold the same amount of water.
- Write the equation 1 ℓ = 1000 cm^3 on the board.

$$10 \text{ cm} \times 10 \text{ cm} \times 10 \text{ cm} = 1000 \text{ cm}^3$$

$$1\ \ell = 1000 \text{ cm}^3$$

- Ask students if 1000 cm^3 is the same as 1 m^3 (since 1000 cm = 1 m). It is not. A cubic meter is 100 cm on the side (not 10, as in the thousand-cube), so its volume is 100 cm × 100 cm × 100 cm = 1,000,000 cm^3, which is 1000 liters. Thus it is not true that 1000 cm^3 = 1 m^3 = 1 liter.

2. Find the height of water in a cuboid container when given its length and width, or the area of the bottom of the container.
   - Draw and label a cuboid such that the volume will be greater than 1000 cm^3 and ask students to find its volume in liters and milliliters.
   - Tell students that we have a container of the same dimensions and we pour 1 ℓ 600 ml of water in it. Ask students to find the height of the water. Guide them in dividing the volume in cm^3 by the length and the width of the container.
   - Remind students that we can simplify the fraction before dividing.
   - Point out that we could instead first find the area of the base of the container, and then divide the volume of water by that to get the height of the water in the container. So we could find the height of the water if we are given the area of the base, without knowing the actual length and width.

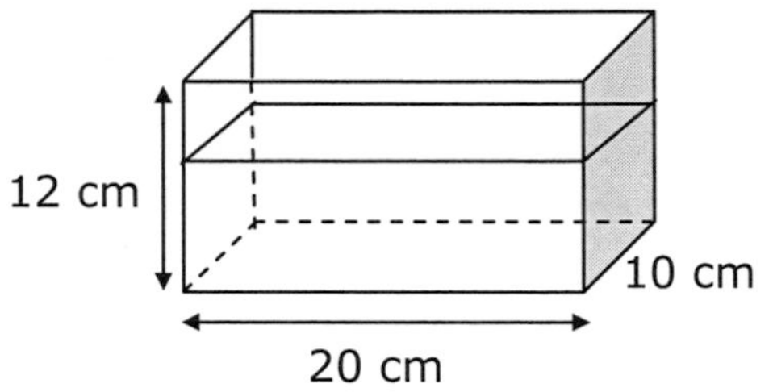

Volume = 20 cm × 10 cm × 12 cm
= 2400 cm^3
= 2400 ml
= 2 ℓ 400 ml

1 ℓ 600 ml = 1600 ml = 1600 cm^3

Height of water = $\frac{1600}{20 \times 10}$

= $\frac{16\not{0}\not{0}}{2\not{0} \times 1\not{0}}$

= 8 cm

3. Discuss **task 4, textbook p. 82.**

Workbook Exercise 53, problems 3-4

Activity 9.1c **Word problems**

1. Discuss **task 6, textbook p. 82**.
   - Since we know the volume of water that was poured out, we can find the decrease in height (3.75 cm). The new height is the different between the original height and the decrease in height.
   - Ask students if they can think of an alternate solution. We can find the volume of water left, and then the height for this volume.
   - You can expand on this problem.
     - Tell students that water was then added to a new height of 7.5 cm. How much water was added?

Decrease in height of water level = $\frac{750}{20 \times 10}$ = 3.75 cm

New height = 10 cm − 3.75 cm = 6.25 cm

Original volume of water = 20 cm × 10 cm × 10 cm
= 2000 cm^3

New volume = 2000 cm^3 − 750 cm^3
= 1250 cm^3

New height = $\frac{1250}{20 \text{ x } 10}$ = 6.25 cm

Change in height = 7.5 cm − 6.25 cm
= 1.25 cm

Volume added = 10 cm × 20 cm × 1.25 cm
= 250 cm^3

- Now, water started leaking at a rate of 3 ml per hour. How long before the tank is empty?

New volume = $1250 \text{ cm}^3 + 250 \text{ cm}^3$
= 1500 cm^3

Or:

New volume = $20 \text{ cm} \times 10 \text{ cm} \times 7.5 \text{ cm}$
= 1500 cm^3

3 ml $\longrightarrow$ 1 h

1500 ml $\longrightarrow \frac{1}{3} \times 1500$
= 500 h
= 20 days 20 h

2. Provide some additional problems for discussion. Have students make sketches of box-shaped containers and label them with the information you give them in the problems. For example:

   - A tank with a base of 20 cm by 30 cm and height of 33 cm is filled with water to a height of 18 cm. How much more water is needed to fill the tank completely? (9 liters)

   - An empty tank has a base 220 cm by 160 cm and a height of 100 cm. The tank is filled with water from two taps each at a rate of 16 liters per minute. How long will it take to fill the tank completely? (110 minutes or 1 h 50 min)

   - A box-shaped container has a base 16 cm by 11 cm and a height of 36 cm. It is partly filled with water to a height of 12 cm. How much water has to be poured out so that it is only one quarter full? (528 ml)

   - Container A is 24 cm long, 10 cm wide and 40 cm high. It is one quarter filled with water. Container B is 30 cm long and 20 cm wide. It is filled with water to a height of 16 cm. When all the water in container A is added to the water in container B, container B is two thirds full. What is the height of container B? (30 cm)

Workbook Exercise 54

Part 2: Finding the Volume of a Solid — 3 sessions

Objectives

- Find the volume of an irregular solid.
- Solve word problems involving displacement of water by solids.

Materials

- Graduated cylinders
- Colored water
- Liquid measuring set
- Objects that sink, e.g. marbles, ball bearings, nuts and bolts, washers, stones

Homework

- Workbook Exercise 55

Notes

So far, students have been finding the volume of cubes and cuboids. Here they will find the volume of solids by using the displacement of a liquid by a solid.

When an object is submerged in water, it displaces a volume of water that is equal to its own volume. The water will rise to a new height. We can use this change in height to find the volume of the object.

Activity 9.2a **Displacement of liquid**

1. Investigate displacement of liquid by a solid.
    - Show students a stone or other irregular solid. Ask them for suggestions on how we can find the volume of the object.
    - Tell students to imagine that they have filled a portable swimming pool all the way to the rim. Then they get in. What happens to the water? It overflows.
    - Provide each group with a 100 ml graduated cylinder. Or, you can do this as a demonstration. Pour 30 ml of water into the cylinder. Add the stone to the cylinder. Lead students to see that the water rises to a new high. Both the water and the stone occupy space. The space that the stone occupies is equivalent to its volume. When the stone is put into the water, it takes up space previously occupied by the water so the water level rises. The amount it rises can be measured and gives us the volume of the stone.
    - If you do not have a graduated cylinder, you can use a beaker or some other container marked in milliliters. Students will still see the effect of the water rising. You can also use an unmarked container, such as a glass, place it in another container, such as a bowl, fill it to the brim with water, and then add an object. The overflow is caught in the bowl and can be measured.
    - Refer to **textbook p. 83** and have students carry out a similar activity, or demonstrate it. Depending on the size of your marbles or other object, fewer or more objects will be needed to displace 30 ml of water. Use uniform objects.
    - After students have found the volume of all the marbles or objects, ask students to find the volume of one object only. Here, the volume of one marble is 3.75 cm^3.
    - If possible, allow students the opportunity to find the volume of some other appropriate objects.

Activity 9.2b **Volume of solids**

1. Discuss learning **tasks 1-3, textbook p. 84**.

2. Provide some additional problems for discussion. Have students make sketches and label them with the information given in the problems. They may also use bar models to solve these problems. For example:

    - A box-shaped container is 20 cm long and 15 cm wide. It is filled with water to a depth of 20 cm. When a stone of volume 600 cm^3 is placed in the tank, the water level rises. What is the height of the new water level? (22 cm)

    - A box-shaped container is 25 cm long and 20 cm wide. It is filled with water to a depth of 18 cm. When a stone is placed in the tank, the water level rises to 22 cm. What is the volume of the stone? (2000 cm^3)

    - A tank measures 90 cm by 50 cm by 70 cm. Five cubes of edge 20 cm are placed in the container. The tank is filled to the brim with water. The water is then drained out from a tap at a rate of 25 liters per minute. How long will it take to empty the tank? (11 minutes)

- A box-shaped container is 20 cm long and 20 cm wide. It is filled with water until it is $\frac{1}{2}$ full. When a metal ball of volume 5600 cm^3 is placed in the container, it becomes $\frac{5}{6}$ full. What is the height of the container? (42 cm. Change in height = $\frac{5600}{20 \times 20}$ = 14 cm. Since the height goes from $\frac{3}{6}$ full to $\frac{5}{6}$ full, then $\frac{2}{6}$ of the height, or $\frac{1}{3}$, is 14 cm. The total height of the container is 14 cm $\times$ 3 = 42 cm.)
- Three identical cubes of edge 20 cm are placed in an empty tank. The width and the height of the tank are 80 cm. The tank is then filled with water from a tap at a rate of 8 liters per minute. It takes 77 minutes to fill up the tank. What is the length of the tank? (100 cm. Volume of 1 cubes = 8000 cm^3. Volume of 3 cubes = 24,000 cm^3. Volume of water added = 77 $\times$ 8000 cm^3 = 616,000 cm^3. Total volume = 24000 cm^3 + 616,000 cm^3 = 640,000 cm^3. Length = $\frac{640,000}{80 \times 80}$ =100 cm.)
- Eight identical metal balls are place in an empty tank measuring 80 cm by 100 cm by 60 cm. The volume of each ball is 12000 cm^3. The container is then filled with water from a tap at a rate of 8 liters per minute. How long will it take to fill the container completely? (48 minutes)

Workbook Exercise 55

Activity 9.2c **Practice**

1. Have students do the problems in **Practice 9A, textbook p. 85** and then share their solutions. Provide additional problems, such as those from activity 9.1c or 9.2b that have not yet been done.

Review

Objectives

- Review all topics.

Suggested number of sessions: 4

	Objectives	Textbook	Workbook	Activities
Review A				**5 sessions**
69 70 71 72	▪ Review.	pp. 86-89, Review C pp. 90-93, Review D US pp. 94-96, Review E	Review 3	R.c

---

Activity R.c **Review**

1. Have students do problems from **Reviews C, D, and E, textbook pp. 86-96.**
   - Students should share their solutions, particularly for the word problems. Possible solutions for selected problems are shown here.

Workbook Review 3

Review C

5. ? 240

5 units = \$240

1 unit = $\$\frac{240}{5}$

8 units = $\$\frac{240}{5} \times 8 = \$48 \times 8 = \$384$

Or:

$\frac{5}{8}$ of total = \$240, so $\frac{8}{8}$ of total = $\$\frac{240}{5} \times 8 = \$384$

11. 40 girls ? girls with glasses

10 units = 40

1 unit = $\frac{40}{10} = 4$

3 units = $4 \times 3 = 12$

12 girls do not wear glasses.

Or:

Number of girls = $\frac{2}{5} \times 40 = 16$

Number of girls that do not wear glasses = $\frac{3}{4}$ of 16 = $\frac{3}{4} \times 16 = 3 \times 4 = 12$

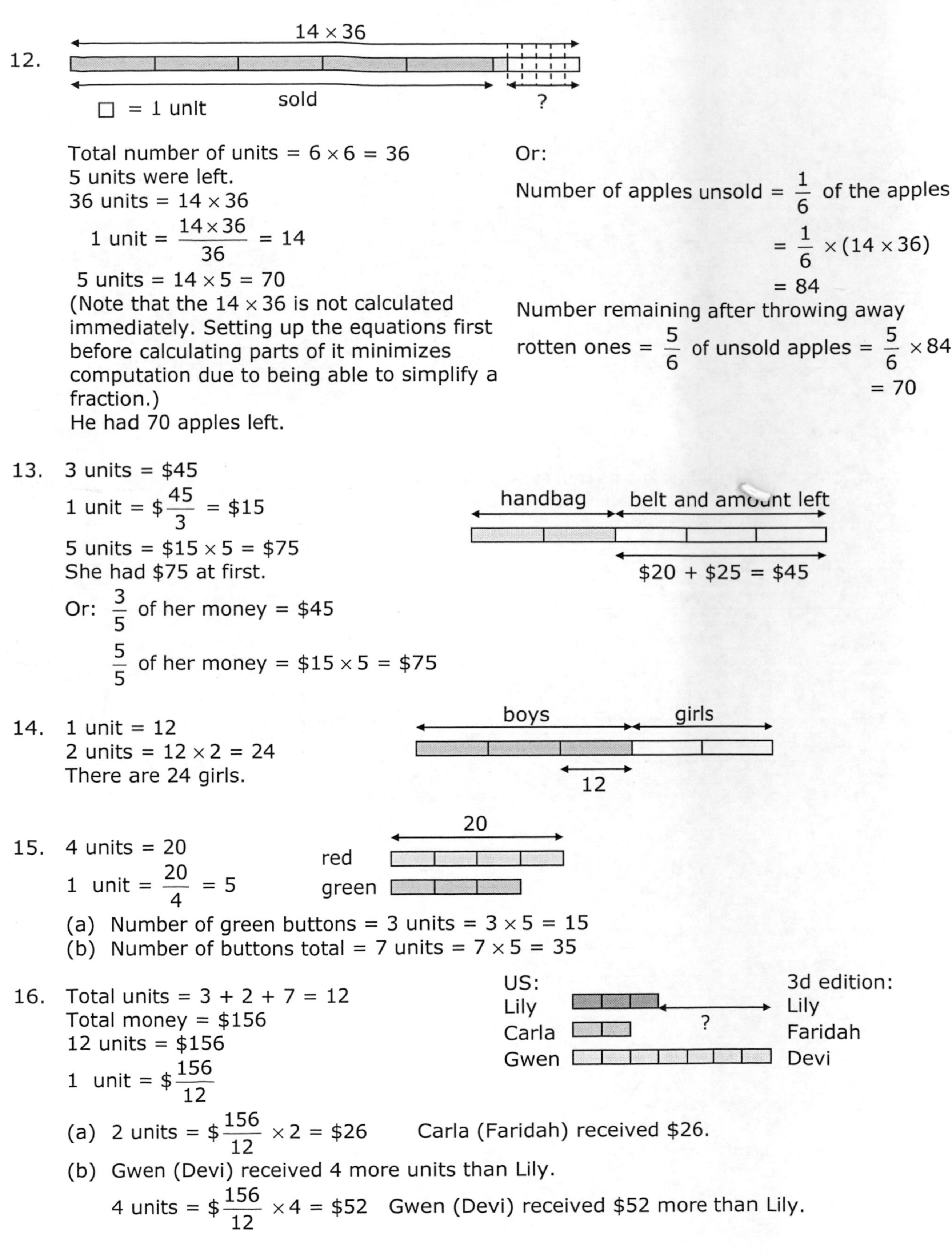

12.

Total number of units = $6 \times 6 = 36$
5 units were left.
36 units = 14×36

1 unit = $\frac{14 \times 36}{36} = 14$

5 units = $14 \times 5 = 70$

(Note that the 14×36 is not calculated immediately. Setting up the equations first before calculating parts of it minimizes computation due to being able to simplify a fraction.)

He had 70 apples left.

Or:

Number of apples unsold = $\frac{1}{6}$ of the apples

$= \frac{1}{6} \times (14 \times 36)$

$= 84$

Number remaining after throwing away rotten ones = $\frac{5}{6}$ of unsold apples = $\frac{5}{6} \times 84$

$= 70$

13. 3 units = \$45

1 unit = $\$\frac{45}{3} = \$15$

5 units = $\$15 \times 5 = \$75$

She had \$75 at first.

Or: $\frac{3}{5}$ of her money = \$45

$\frac{5}{5}$ of her money = $\$15 \times 5 = \$75$

14. 1 unit = 12

2 units = $12 \times 2 = 24$

There are 24 girls.

15. 4 units = 20

1 unit = $\frac{20}{4} = 5$

(a) Number of green buttons = 3 units = $3 \times 5 = 15$
(b) Number of buttons total = 7 units = $7 \times 5 = 35$

16. Total units = 3 + 2 + 7 = 12

Total money = \$156

12 units = \$156

1 unit = $\$\frac{156}{12}$

(a) 2 units = $\$\frac{156}{12} \times 2 = \$26$ Carla (Faridah) received \$26.

(b) Gwen (Devi) received 4 more units than Lily.

4 units = $\$\frac{156}{12} \times 4 = \$52$ Gwen (Devi) received \$52 more than Lily.

28. (a) Total liters needed = $50 \times 30 \times 20 = 30{,}000\ \text{cm}^3 = 30\ \ell$

(b) $12\ \ell \longrightarrow 1$ min

$1\ \ell \longrightarrow \frac{1}{12}$ min

$30\ \ell \longrightarrow \frac{1}{12} \times 30$ min $= 2\frac{1}{2}$ min

It will take $2\frac{1}{2}$ min to fill the tank.

Review D

13.

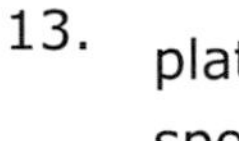

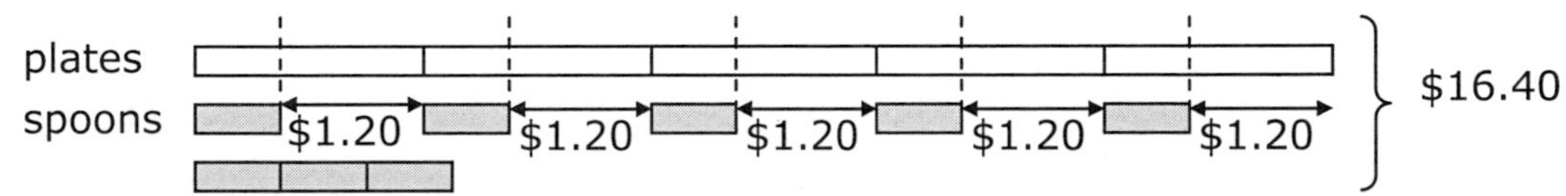

Each plate is $1.20 more than a spoon. So if $1.20 were removed from the price of each of the 5 plates, then the resulting price would be the cost of 5 spoons. The total cost would then be the cost of 8 + 5 = 13 spoons.

13 units = $16.40 - (5 × $1.20) = $10.40

1 unit = $\$\frac{10.40}{13} = \$0.80$

Each spoon cost $0.80.

15. Total weight of both boys = $48\ \text{kg} \times 2 = 96$ kg

If 6 kg is added to the weight, both would weigh the same as the heavier boy.

96 + 6 = 102 kg

Weight of heavier boy = $\frac{102}{2}$ kg = 51 kg

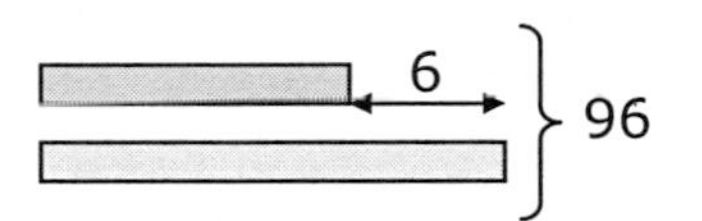

16.

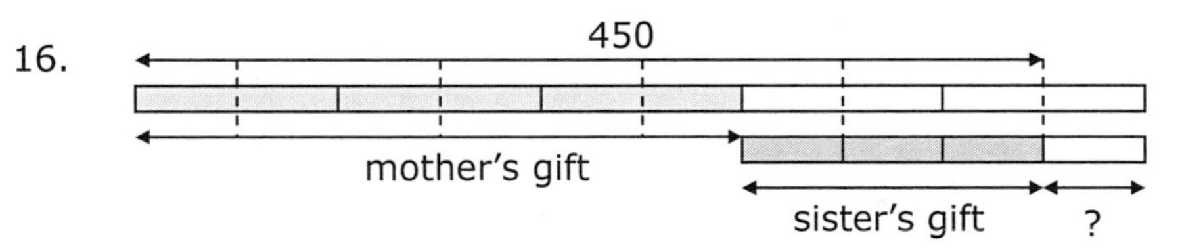

(a) Total number of units = 10

He spent $\frac{3}{10}$ of his money on his sister's present.

Or:

$\frac{3}{4}$ of remainder = $\frac{3}{4} \times \frac{2}{5} = \frac{3}{10}$

(b) 9 units = $450

1 unit = $50

He had $50 left.

Total spent = $\frac{3}{5} + \frac{3}{10} = \frac{6+3}{10} = \frac{9}{10}$

$\frac{9}{10}$ of total = $450

$\frac{1}{10}$ of total = $50

19. 2 units = 12

$1 \text{ unit} = \frac{12}{2} = 6$

12 units = $6 \times 12 = 72$

There are 72 members altogether.

men
women
12

20. Percent of total girls = 100% - 60% = 40%

20% of total is how many more boys than girls there are.

$20\% \text{ of } 1800 = \frac{20}{100} \times 1800 = 360$

There are **360** more boys than girls.

21. (a) $\angle BAC = 180° - (2 \times 58°) = 64°$ — Angle sum of Δ, isosceles Δ

$58° + (64° + y) + 26° = 180°$ — Angle sum of Δ

$y = 180° - 58° - 64° - 26° = 32°$

(b) $\angle CDB = 180° - 145° = 35°$ — Adjacent $\angle$s on a straight line

$y = 62° + 35° = 97°$ — Exterior angle of a Δ

22. Side of the square = 8 cm ($8 \times 8 = 64$)

Height of triangle = 8 cm

Area of triangle = $\frac{1}{2} \times 8 \times 10 = 40 \text{ cm}^2$

US edition: Review E

6. $\frac{5}{6} \longrightarrow 10$ gal

$\frac{1}{6} \longrightarrow 10 \div 5 = 2$ gal

$\frac{6}{6} \longrightarrow 2 \text{ gal} \times 6 = 12$ gal

13. (a) $2 \text{ yd } 2 \text{ ft} \times 5 = (2 \text{ yd} \times 5) + (2 \text{ ft} \times 5)$

$= 10 \text{ yd} + 10 \text{ ft}$

$= 10 \text{ yd} + 3 \text{ yd} + 1 \text{ ft}$

$= 13 \text{ yd } 1 \text{ ft}$

(e) $5 \text{ lb } 12 \text{ oz} \div 4 = (4 \text{ lb} + 16 \text{ oz} + 12 \text{ oz}) \div 4$

$= (4 \text{ lb} \div 4) + (28 \text{ oz} \div 4)$

$= 1 \text{ lb } 7 \text{ oz}$

18. $\frac{2}{5} \rightarrow 14$ gal

$\frac{1}{5} \rightarrow 14 \text{ gal} \div 2 = 7$ gal

$\frac{5}{5} \rightarrow 7 \text{ gal} \times 5 = 35$ gal

Workbook Review 3

15. $\angle ACB + 35° + 40° = 90°$ — right-angled triangle BCD
    $\angle ACB = 90° - 35° - 40° = 15°$
    $\angle BAC + \angle ACB = 90°$
    $\angle BAC = 90° - \angle ACB = 90° - 15° = 75°$ — right-angled triangle ABC

16. $\angle QRS = 180° - 74° = 106°$ — Sum of pairs of $\angle$s between two // lines =180°
    $\angle TRS = 74°$
    $\angle QRT = 106° - 74° = 32°$ — Isosceles triangle TRS

20.

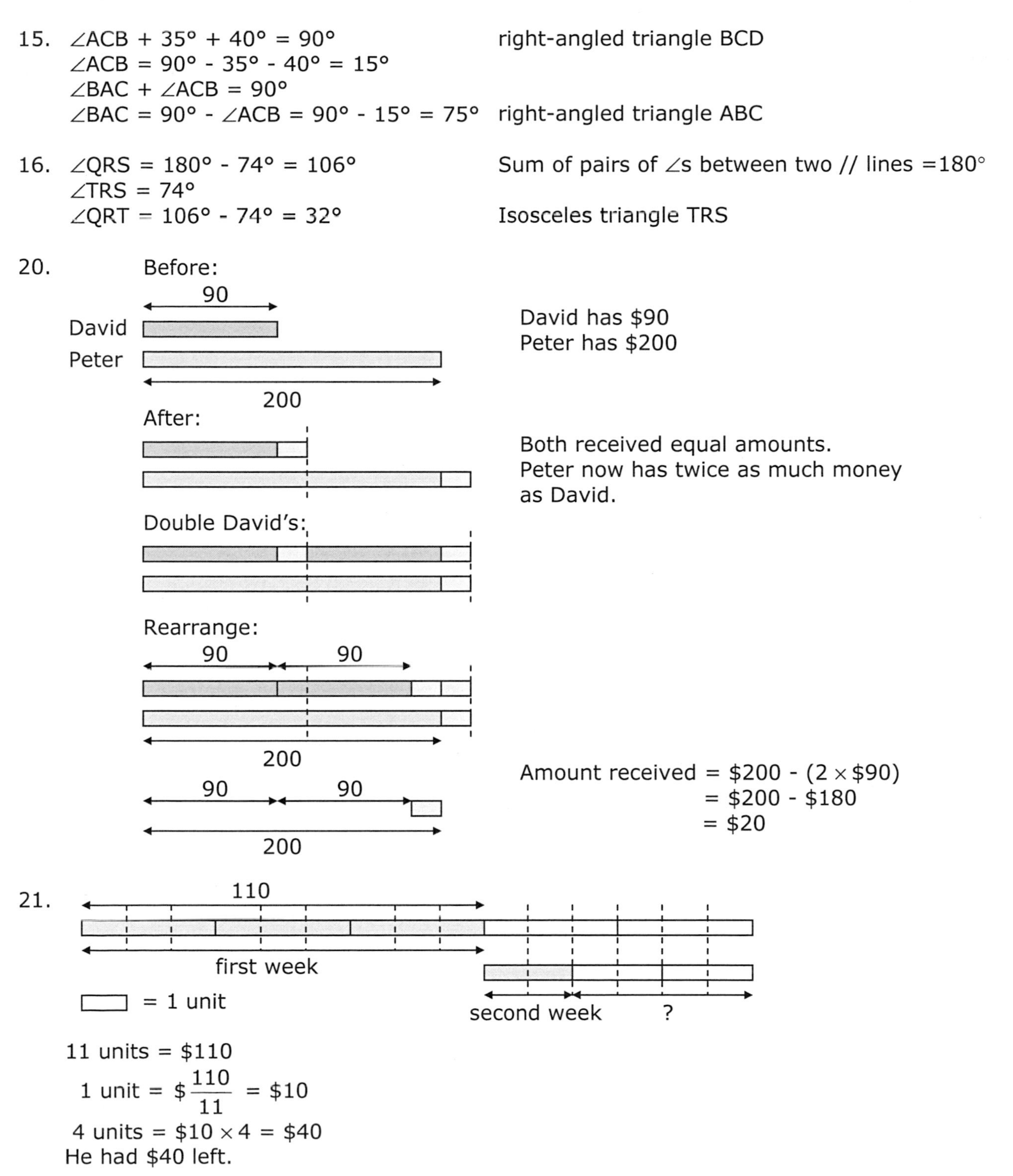

David has $90
Peter has $200

Both received equal amounts.
Peter now has twice as much money as David.

Amount received = $200 - (2 × $90)
= $200 - $180
= $20

21.

11 units = $110

1 unit = $ $\frac{110}{11}$ = $10

4 units = $10 × 4 = $40

He had $40 left.

Textbook Answer Key

Unit 1 – Decimals

Part 1: Approximation and Estimation (pp. 6-7)

1. 3.15, 3.14, 3.15
2. (a) 5.17 (b) 8.04
(c) 10.81 (d) 23.72
4. (a) 0.09 (b) 8.96
(c) 1.21 (d) 6.92
(e) 6.92 (f) 6.98
5. 0.67, 4.67
6. (a) 0.43 (b) 0.63
(c) 0.22 (d) 0.17
(e) 5.78 (f) 1.33
(g) 4.71 (h) 8.38

Part 2: Multiplication by Tens, Hundreds or Thousands (pp. 8-11)

1. (a) 6 (b) 8 (c) 9
(d) 0.2 (e) 0.4 (f) 0.3
(g) 0.05 (h) 0.06 (i) 0.07
4. (a) 1.2 (b) 0.68 (c) 3.45
(d) 20.5 (e) 32.1 (f) 14.39
(g) 75 (h) 104 (i) 118
5. 21.2
6. (a) 0.18 (b) 3.2 (c) 45
(d) 6.4 (e) 476.7 (d) 194.88
7. 0.7
9. 6
11. (a) 0.3 (b) 320 (c) 132.5
(d) 90 (e) 3620 (f) 13,400
12. 840.6
13. 8406
14. (a) 2.4 (b) 72 (c) 616
(d) 150 (e) 1500 (f) 20,480

Part 3: Division by Tens, Hundreds, or Thousands (pp. 12-15)

1. (a) 0.8 (b) 0.08 (c) 0.008
(d) 0.2 (e) 0.02 (f) 0.002
(g) 0.6 (h) 0.06 (i) 0.006
4. (a) 0.023 (b) 0.045 (c) 0.012
(d) 0.25 (e) 0.68 (f) 0.53
(g) 1.2 (h) 3.9 (i) 10.3
5. 0.07
6. (a) 0.2 (b) 0.2 (c) 0.7
(d) 0.08 (e) 0.017 (f) 0.043
7. 0.04
9. 0.005
11. (a) 0.08 (b) 0.9 (c) 0.015
(d) 0.004 (e) 0.2 (f) 0.324
12. 0.23
13. 0.023
14. (a) 0.004 (b) 0.004 (c) 0.016
(d) 0.002 (e) 0.013 (f) 0.102

Part 4: Multiplication by a 2-Digit Whole Number (pp. 16-17)

1. (a) 90,000 (b) 9000 (c) 900
3. (a) 33.54 (b) 12.19 (c) 181.3
(d) 616.2 (e) 1827 (f) 2383.2
(g) 153.94 (h) 392.34 (i) 113.04

Part 5: Conversion of Measurements (pp. 18-20)

1. (a) 75 (b) 375 US (c) 6
2. (a) 2800 US (b) 100
3. (a) 60 (b) 490
(c) 615 (d) 300
(e) 1850 (f) 4200
(g) 250 (h) 1050
US (i) 11 US (j) 56
US (k) 39 US (l) 2
4. 200
5. (a) 4 m 60 cm (b) 7 km 400 m
(c) 1 kg 200 g (d) 5 ℓ 900 ml
(e) 3 km 450 m
(f) 2 m 6 cm (g) 4 ℓ 5 ml
(h) 6 kg 432 g
US (i) 4 lb 4 oz US (j) 7 ft 6 in.
6. 0.145
7. (a) 0.35 (b) 0.42
(c) 0.625 (d) 0.3
9. 3.5
10. (a) 4.35 (b) 5.09 (c) 2.8
(d) 4.075 US (e) 3.75 US (f) 3.5
11. 3.080
12. (a) 4.070 (b) 2.380 (c) 5.200
(d) 6.05 US (e) 4.25 US (f) 5.5

Practice 1A (p. 21)

1. (a) 0.12 (b) 7.51
(c) 40.08 (d) 81.14
(e) 0.73 (f) 3.12
(g) 59.01 (h) 18.61
2. (a) 6.27 km (b) 4.08 kg
(c) 0.19 ℓ (d) 20.25 ℓ

3. (a) 0.13 (b) 0.57
   (c) 2.56 (d) 5.67
4. (a) 57 (b) 150.8 (c) 7250
5. (a) 0.06 (b) 1316 (c) 20,400
6. (a) 10.92 (b) 115.92 (c) 37.41
7. (a) 3.9 (b) 0.342 (c) 0.009
8. (a) 3.3 (b) 1.08 (c) 0.03
9. (a) 285 ml
   (b) US 3 qt 3d *85 m*
   (c) US 85 m 3d *706 g*
   US (d) 3 in. US (e) 706 g
   US (f) 8 oz
10. (a) 0.67 ℓ
    (b) US 0.75 lb 3d *0.105 km*
    (c) US 0.105 km 3d *0.069 kg*
    US (d) 0.75 qt US (e) 0.069 kg
    US (f) 0.5 ft
11. (a) 20 km 80 m
    (b) US 3 qt 3 c 3d *16 ℓ 500 ml*
    (c) US 16 ℓ 500 ml 3d *2 kg 80 g*
    US (d) 18 ft 6 in.
    US (e) 2 kg 80 g
    US (f) 4 lb 12 oz
12. (a) 9.6 m
    (b) US 27 qt 3d *4.705 ℓ*
    (c) US 4.705 ℓ 3d *25.006 km*
    US (d) 37 oz
    US (c) 25.006 km
    US (d) 43 in.
13. 1.58 m
14. 1.95 kg

Review A (pp. 22-24)

1. (a) 0.005 (b) 50,000 (c) 0.05
2. (a) 50.806 (b) 7.031
   (c) 45.308 (d) 8.009
3. (a) 12.61 (b) 9.9
4. (a) 31,238; 31,328; 31,823; 31,832
   (b) $4\frac{1}{6}$; $4\frac{3}{10}$; $4\frac{2}{5}$; $\frac{9}{2}$
   (c) 4.089; 4.98; 498; 4,809
   (d) 2.05; $2\frac{1}{2}$; 2.51; $2\frac{3}{5}$
5. (a) 8.4 (b) 5.75 (c) 1.875
6. (a) 0.43 (b) 0.22 (c) 0.83
7. (a) $\frac{31}{500}$ (b) $2\frac{9}{25}$ (c) $6\frac{77}{250}$
8. (a) 1,200,000
   (b) 18,120 (c) 201.5
   (d) 24 (e) 0.489 (f) 3.25
9. (a) 207 (b) 72
   (c) 68 (d) 185
10. (a) 30 (b) $7\frac{1}{2}$ (c) $\frac{7}{45}$
11. (a) 2 kg 60 g (b) 1,730 m
    (c) 0.5 m (d) 2.008 ℓ
    (e) 30 min (f) 26 months
    (g) 5750 m (h) 8 ℓ 375 ml
12. $522.50
13. 0.725 kg
14. 2.1 m
15. $9.10
16. $\frac{1}{2}$
17. $\frac{1}{8}$ ℓ
18. 768
19. 128
20. Width = 15 m; Perimeter = 70 m
21. 60 cm; 108 cm^2
22. 65 cm^2
23. 24 cm^2
24. (a) 53° (b) 118°

Unit 2 – Percentage

Part 1: Percent (pp. 25-27)

1. 27%
2. (a) 67% (b) 50%
   (c) 9% (d) 100%
3. (a) 33% (b) 20% (c) 5%
4. (a) 23% (b) 45%
   (c) 36% (d) 75%
   (e) 40% (f) 70%
   (g) 30% (h) 50%
5. 35%
6. (a) 7% (b) 2%
   (c) 85% (d) 70%
7. 0.43
8. (a) 0.28 (b) 0.88
   (c) 0.30 (d) 0.05
9. $\frac{2}{5}$
10. (a) $\frac{1}{10}$ (b) $\frac{4}{5}$
    (c) $\frac{1}{4}$ (d) $\frac{3}{4}$
    (e) $\frac{1}{20}$ (f) $\frac{2}{25}$
    (g) $\frac{1}{25}$ (e) $\frac{1}{50}$

Part 2: Writing Fractions as Percentages (pp. 28-31)

75%
1. (a) 40% (b) 50%
2. 28%
3. 70%
4. (a) 25% (b) 40%
(c) 80% (d) 45%
(e) 65% (f) 24%
(g) 56% (h) 82%
5. 60%
6. 49%
7. (a) 4% (b) 18%
(c) 20% (d) 43%
(e) 10% (f) 32%
(g) 4% (h) 51%
8. (a) 10% (b) 50% (c) 80%
(d) 70% (e) 40%
9. (a) 75% (b) 25%
10. (a) 28% (b) 72%
11. (a) 60%

Practice 2A (p. 32)

1. (a) 25% (b) 5%
(c) 70% (d) 36%
(e) 75% (f) 55%
(g) 50% (h) 60%
(i) 48% (j) 20%
(k) 20% (l) 5%
2. (a) 63% (b) 5%
(c) 20% (d) 50%
3. (a) $\frac{23}{50}$ (b) $\frac{1}{20}$
(c) $\frac{7}{100}$ (d) $\frac{4}{5}$
4. (a) 0.15 (b) 0.41
(c) 0.09 (d) 0.5
5. 15%
6. 63%
7. $\frac{3}{5}$
8. 30%
9. 80%
10. 28%
11. 90%
12. 70%
13. 60%

Part 3: Percentage of a Quantity (pp. 33-36)

150
1. 108
2. 24
3. (a) 15 (b) 16 (c) 10 kg
(d) 10 m (e) 31.5 km (f) 300 g
4. (a) 40 (b) 200
5. 352
6. $81; $2,781
7. $108; $792
8. $120; $1620
9. 20; 380

Practice 2B (p. 37)

1. (a) 6.56 (b) $121.50
(c) 33 (d) 123.2
(e) 111 kg (f) 322.4 m
2. 540
3. 4.2 m^2
4. 45
5. 9
6. $405
7. 756
8. $51.50
9. $133
10. $3605
11. 9
12. 84
13. 30

Unit 3 – Average

Part 1: Average (pp. 38-42)

1. 5
2. 5
3. 114; 38
4. (a) 11 m (b) 2.2 m
5. (a) 310 (b) 77.5
6. 237 km
7. 373
8. $37.20
9. 4 kg 200 g
10. 1 kg 300 g
11. 7 min 40 s
12. 8 min 15 s
13. 1.48 m
14. $5.70

Practice 3A (p. 43)

1. (a) 26.3 (b) \$2.81
   (c) 4.1 kg (d) 5.15 ℓ
   (e) 2.39 m (f) 19.4 km
   [US] (g) 3.48 gal [US] (h) 7.77 in.
2. 1820 km
3. 108 kg
4. \$15
5. 6 h 40 min
6. 3 ℓ 425 ml
7. \$2.10
8. 160

Unit 4 - Rate

Part 1: Rate (pp. 44-49)

2. 25
3. 720
4. 150
5. (a) 125 (b) 4
6. 3
7. (a) 180 (b) 10
8. 15
9. 9
10. 84; 76; 160
11. (a) 0.70 (b) 1.80; 2.50
12. 2, 4.40

Practice 4A (p. 50)

1. 50 min
2. 4
3. 2280
4. 50 min
5. \$1485
6. 80 m
7. (a) \$0.50 (b) \$1.50
8. (a) \$220 (b) \$520

Unit 5 - Line Graphs

Part 1: Line Graphs (pp. 51-53)

(a) 1000 (b) 1500 (c) 500
1. (a) 75 (b) 100
2. (a) \$150,000 (b) \$125,000
3. (a) 18 (b) 5 (c) 8

Review B (pp. 54-56)

1. (a) 22 (b) 40
   (c) 460 (d) 32
2. 82
3. 60
4. $\frac{1}{4}$ kg
5. \$1500
6. 48 cm
7. \$17.50
8. 1.71 m
9. (a) 75% (b) 70%
10. 0.80
11. $\frac{9}{25}$
12. (a) 90% (b) 8%
    (c) 58% (d) 9%
13. (a) 11.2 (b) 78.4 kg
    (c) \$3.15
14. 147
15. 25
16. 5200
17. \$36
18. 40 min
19. \$28.40
20. 72 cm^2
21. [US] 20 $in.^2$ [3d] *20* cm^2
22. (a) 30° (b) 20°
23. (a) 200 ℓ (b) \$115.50

Unit 6 – Triangles

Part 1: Sum of Angles of a Triangle

1. (a) 90 + 55 + 35 = 180
   (b) 75 + 65 + 40 = 180
   (c) 35 + 125 + 20 = 180
2. 44
3. (a) 68 (b) 102 (c) 43
5. 33
6. A and C
8. 84
9. (a) 133 (b) 60

Part 2: Isosceles and Equilateral Triangles (pp. 61-64)

3. B and C
4. P and Q
5. 110
6. 130
7. 75
8. (a) 130 (b) 40
   (c) 120 (d) 30 (e) 20

Unit 7 - 4-Sided Figures

Part 1: Parallelograms, Rhombuses, and Trapezoids (pp. 68-71)

3. (x) 80 (y) 60 (z) 65
4. (x) 60 (y) 50 (z) 55
5. 130; 60
6. (a) 55 (b) 112 (c) 108

Unit 9 - Volume

Part 1: Cubes and Cuboids (pp. 80-82)

1. 3
2. 4
3. (a) 9 (b) 12
4. 12.5
5. (a) 4 (b) 4
6. 3.75; 6.25

Part 2: Finding the Volume of a Solid (pp. 83-84)

80, 30
1. 1,800; 1,800
2. 1,080

Practice 9A (p. 85)

1. (a) 4 cm (b) US 9 in. 3d *9 cm*
2. US 5 in. 3d *5 cm*
3. 12.5 cm
4. 6 cm
5. 108 cm^3

Review C (pp. 86-89)

1. (a) 2250 g (b) 3.09 km
   (c) 2 m 30 cm
2. 8:55 p.m.
3. $\frac{1}{10}$
4. $9
5. $384
6. 12
7. (a) 145 (b) 3.15 cm
8. 68
9. (a) 1 : 5 (b) 1 : 2 (c) 3 : 2
   (d) 4 : 1 (e) 5 : 2 (f) 1 : 25
10. (a) 15 (b) 8
11. 12
12. 70
13. $75
14. 24
15. (a) 15 (b) 35
16. (a) $26 (b) $52
17. 480
18. $227.50
19. $3060
20. $704
21. 81 cm^2
22. 20 m^2
23. 630 cm^2
24. 32°
25. 12,000 cm^3
26. 7.5 cm
27. 3 kg
28. (a) 30 ℓ (b) $2\frac{1}{2}$ min.

Review D (pp. 90-93)

1. (a) 18 (b) 36
2. (a) $2\frac{1}{3}$ (b) 63
   (c) $\frac{1}{4}$ (d) $\frac{4}{27}$
3. (a) 3.79 (b) 0.867
4. $2\frac{9}{200}$
5. (a) 4.0 (b) 7.64
6. 3000 km
7. 106
8. 5 : 3 : 14
9. (a) 80% (b) 45%
10. $\frac{12}{25}$
11. 156 min
12. 0.75 kg
13. $0.80
14. $23.33
15. 51 kg
16. (a) $\frac{3}{10}$ (b) $50
17. 24 min
18. $4.90
19. 72
20. 360
21. (a) 32° (b) 97°
22. 40 cm^2
23. 12 cm
24. 8 ℓ
25. (a) (b) 52%

***Review E (pp. 94-96)**

1. 548
2. (a) $\frac{7}{12}$ lb (b) $1\frac{1}{3}$ lb
3. $\frac{3}{10}$ qt
4. $1\frac{1}{4}$ ft
5. 6 mi
6. 12 gal
7. 30 in.
8. (a) 11 oz; $\frac{3}{4}$ lb; $\frac{13}{16}$ lb
   (b) 1.5 gal; 10 qt; 16 qt
   (c) $3\frac{1}{6}$ ft; 39 in.; $1\frac{2}{3}$ yd
9.

	Height	Weight
Ryan	21.5 in.	7 lb 3 oz
Alex	19 in.	6 lb 2 oz
Jeff	20.5 in.	6 lb 12 oz.

10. 143 in.
11. 245.68 ft
12. 2 lb 9 oz
13. (a) 13 yd 1 ft (b) 40 gal 2 qt
    (c) 38 qt 2 c (d) 26 qt 0 pt
    (e) 1 lb 7 oz (f) 0 ft 4 in.
    (g) 1 gal 1 qt
14. 11 in.
15. (a) 60 in.^{2} (b) 48 ft^2
16. (a) 120 in.^{3} (b) 14 ft^3
17. 15 in.
18. 35 gal
19. (a) 23 qt (b) 59 in.
    (c) 93 oz (d) 8 pt
20. (a) 3 qt 3 c (b) 22 qt 1 pt
    (c) 52 gal 0 qt (d) 3 ft 2 in.

Workbook Answer Key

Exercise 1

1. (a) 5.97 (b) 21.50 (c) 17.01
2. 0.08 2.31 4.08 3.26 1.80
   0.01 3.02 4.04 3.66 1.21

Exercise 2

1. (a) 7.78 (b) 4.50 (c) 4.34
   (d) 6.92 (e) 0.08 (f) 3.01
2. 4.48 m
3. US 1.15 lb 3d 1.15 *kg*

Exercise 3

1. (a) 0.89 (b) 0.43 (c) 0.67
   (d) 4.17 (e) 5.63 (f) 9.14

Exercise 4

1. (a) 0.3 (b) 0.09
   (c) 0.67 (d) 8.4
   (e) 29 (f) 3.21
   (g) 52.4 (h) 354
   (i) 60.15 (j) 4128
2. (a) 1.8 (b) 128
   (c) 277.8
   (d) 1832 (e) 1116

Exercise 5

1. 3.24 32.4 324
   16.35 163.5 1635
   30.04 300.4 3004
   81.9 819 8190
   204 2040 20,400
2. (a) 616.6 (b) 200.9
   (c) 520.1 (d) 306.5
   (e) 72 (f) 8625
   (g) 4860 (h) 3700
3. (a) 10 (b) 10 (c) 100
   (d) 1000 (e) 10
   (f) 1000 (g) 1000 (h) 100
   (i) 100 (j) 1000

Exercise 6

1. (a) 12 (b) 102
   (c) 2720 (d) 1560
   (e) 387,000 (f) 224,560
   (g) 76,320 (h) 29,160

Exercise 7

1. (a) 0.6 (b) 0.03
   (c) 0.005 (d) 0.034
   (e) 0.12 (f) 1.9
   (g) 2.05 (h) 0.365
   (i) 23.9 (j) 0.058
2. (a) 0.04 (b) 0.074 (c) 0.089
   (d) 0.912 (e) 0.423

Exercise 8

1. 20.3 2.03 0.203
   0.8 0.08 0.008
   705 70.5 7.05
   5.8 0.58 0.058
   145.8 14.58 1.458
2. (a) 0.54 (b) 0.203
   (c) 28.2 (d) 0.034
   (e) 4.525 (f) 3.4
   (g) 0.073 (h) 0.002
3. (a) 10 (b) 100
   (c) 1000 (d) 100
   (e) 1000 (f) 10
   (g) 100 (h) 1000
   (i) 10 (j) 1000

Exercise 9

1. (a) 0.036 (b) 0.03
   (c) 0.106 (d) 0.072
   (e) 0.003 (f) 0.013
   (g) 0.098 (h) 0.121

Exercise 10

1. (a) 2000 (b) 1200 (c) 1200
   (d) 2100 (e) 2000

Exercise 11

1. (a) 110.4 (b) 240.87
   (c) 1246.44 (d) 31,761
   (e) 50.74 (f) 105.06
   (g) 1498.77 (h) 4834.05
2. 21.6 25.16 73.37
   3122.2 48.76 52.78
   46.5 354.72 1514.88
   watch

Exercise 12

1. (a) 400 (b) 1500
   (c) 90 (d) 43
   (e) US 1 ft 3 in. 3d *1 m 5 cm*
   (f) US 4 lb 12 oz 3d *4 kg 125 g*
   (g) 3 km 40 m
   (h) 3 ℓ 800 ml

Exercise 13

1. (a) 0.006 (b) 0.08
   (c) 0.04 (d) 0.054
   (e) 2.3 (f) 3.5
   (g) 4.03 (h) 2.6

Exercise 14

1. (a) 2.5 (b) 1.08
   (c) 3.006 (d) 2.4
   (e) US 3.5 3d *4.072*
   (f) 3.45
   (g) US 19.25 3d *2.35*
   (h) 3.245

Review 1

1. (a) Seven hundred thousand, two hundred forty-eight
   (b) Two million, one hundred nine thousand, thirty-five
2. (a) 860,709 (b) 3,000,040
3. (a) 7 (b) 4.21
4. (a) 366 (b) 0.537
5. (a) 1, 2, 4, 5, 10, 20, 25, 50, 100
   (b) 9 (c) 40; 80
6. (a) 7000 (b) 30,000
   (c) 400 (d) 100
7. (a) 2.7 (b) 3.08
   (c) 1.6 (d) 1.75
8. $\frac{11}{4}$
9. $2\frac{1}{2}, \frac{5}{3}, \frac{5}{8}, \frac{7}{12}$
10. (a) − (b) +
    (c) x (d) ÷
11. 4,000,000
12. $\frac{1}{2}$
13. (a) 25 (b) 2400
14. (a) 0.58 (b) 4.6 (c) 2.004
15. 786
16. $52.15
17. 14
18. 0.1 m
19. 1.53 m
20. 4 : 13
21. 45 cm^2
22. 84 cm^2
23. 50 cm
24. $4.24
25. 64
26. 36

Exercise 15

1. (a) 7 (b) 15 (c) 29
   (d) 26 (e) 38 (f) 28
3. 87% 5%
   16% 71%
   68% 50%
   99% 100%
4. 7 1
   43 99
   100 100
   100 100

Exercise 16

1. (a) 15% (b) 86% (c) 40%
   (d) 90% (e) 47%
   (f) 12% (g) 4% (h) 50%
   (i) 75% (j) 6%
2. (a) 0.24 (b) 0.37 (c) 0.78
   (d) 0.06 (e) 0.62
   (f) 0.53 (g) 0.1 (h) 0.07
   (i) 0.8 (j) 0.9

Exercise 17

1. (a) $\frac{11}{50}$ (b) $\frac{9}{20}$ (c) $\frac{24}{25}$
   (d) $\frac{13}{25}$ (e) $\frac{3}{50}$
   (f) $\frac{2}{5}$ (g) $\frac{9}{10}$ (h) $\frac{2}{25}$
   (i) $\frac{3}{4}$ (j) $\frac{1}{2}$

Exercise 18

1. (a) 50% (b) 18% (c) 85%
   (d) 48% (e) 60%
   (f) 60% (g) 16% (h) 25%
   (i) 24% (j) 30%
2. (a) 20% (b) 50% (c) 30%
   (d) 35% (e) 60%

Exercise 19

1. (a) 93% (b) 13% (c) 24%
   (d) 47% (e) 61%
2. 45%
3. 30%
4. 32%

Exercise 20

1. (a) 48% (b) 52%
2. (a) 40% (b) 60%
3. (a) 30% (b) 70%
4. (a) 68% (b) 32%

Exercise 21

1. (a) 12 (b) 108 (c) $28.20
   (d) $12.50 (e) 60 m (f) 20 kg
2. $46.75
3. 12
4. $225

Exercise 22

1. 33
2. $588
3. $1,020
4. 135

Exercise 23

1. (a) $108 (b) $1908
2. $3024
3. (a) $12 (b) $48
4. $11.25

Exercise 24

1. $36
2. 1560

Exercise 25

1. (a) 18, 6 (b) 39
   (c) 27 (d) 43
2. 7
3. $26

Exercise 26

1. (a) $4.15 (b) 13.2 m
   (c) 14.6 kg (d) 226 ℓ
2. 4.68 m
3. US 1.34 lb 3d *1.34 kg*

Exercise 27

1. 86
2. 90 g
3. 37.2
4. US 114 in. 3d *114 cm*

Exercise 28

1. (a) 12 m 80 cm
   (b) 255 cm; 2 m 55 cm
   (c) 6 m 255 cm; 8 m 55 cm
2. (a) 10 ℓ 750 ml
   (b) 1,600; 1 ℓ 600 ml
   (c) 12 ℓ 1600 ml; 13 ℓ 600 ml
3. (a) 2 km 125 m
   (b) 400 m
   (c) 1 km 400 m
4. (a) 2 h 15 min
   (b) 20 min
   (c) 1 h 20 min

Exercise 29

1. 2 kg 350 g
2. 13 ℓ 500 ml

Exercise 30

1. 50 kg
2. $4.60

Exercise 31

1. (a) 75 (b) 50
   (c) 12 (d) 34

Exercise 32

1. (a) 225 (b) 7875
   (c) 175 (d) 144

Exercise 33

1. 20 min
2. 5 days
3. $7\frac{1}{2}$
4. $42
5. 1000
6. 15 ℓ

Exercise 34

1. 60 (a) 360 (b) 20
2. 14 (a) 224 (b) 15
3. 40 (a) 3600 (b) 50

4. 150 (a) 2250 (b) 5
5. (a) 120 s (b) 5 days
6. (a) 625 (b) 8 min

Exercise 35

1. (a) $5 (b) $9 (c) $3.50
2. (a) $8.40 (b) $19.20 (c) $33.05

Exercise 36

1. (a) 200 (b) from 1981 to 1982
   (c) 700 (d) 3400 (e) 850
2. (a) Wed. (b) 375 (c) Sat.
   (d) 75 (e) from Tue. to Wed.
3. (a) 3 cm (b) 4 cm
   (c) from Tue. to Wed.
   (d) from Thu. to Fri., 4 cm
   (e) 4 days
4. (a) 7 a.m. (b) 130
   (c) from 8 a.m. to 9 a.m.
   (d) from 7 a.m. to 8 a.m.
   (b) from 9 a.m. to 10 a.m.

Exercise 37

1. (a) 4, 8, 3, 16, 5
   (b) 2.50 (c) 18
2. (a) 3 min (b) $4\frac{1}{2}$ min
   (c) 40 ℓ (d) 70 ℓ

Exercise 38

1. (a) 32° (b) 42°
   (c) 124° (d) 20°

Exercise 39

1. (a) 75° (b) 39°
   (c) 90° (d) 85°

Exercise 40

1. (a) 123° (b) 136°
   (c) 39° (d) 31°

Exercise 41

1. (a) 43° (b) 52°
   (c) 110° (d) 43°

Exercise 42

1. (a) 60° (b) 30°
   (c) 65° (d) 60°

Exercise 43

1. (a) 70° (b) 53°
   (c) 145° (d) 28°
   (e) 62° (f) 120°
   (g) 50° (h) 45°

Exercise 45

1. (a) 55° (b) 105°
   (c) 125° (d) 20°
   (e) 110° (f) 60°
   (g) 100° (h) 135°

Exercise 46

1. (a) 100° (b) 30°
   (c) 56° (d) 107°
   (e) 140° (f) 45°
   (g) 60° (h) 50°

Exercise 47

1. (a) 68° (b) 25°
   (c) 96°, 132° (d) 112°, 68°
   (e) 80° (f) 18°
   (g) 48°, 59° (h) 62°

Exercise 50

1. (a) No (b) Yes
   (c) Yes (d) No

Review 2

1. 0.75 0.35
   $\frac{4}{5}$ $\frac{7}{20}$ $\frac{12}{25}$
   80% 75% 48%
2. (a) 35% (b) 65%
3. 40%
4. (a) $25 (b) $1050
5. $156
6. $184
7. $6.60
8. (a) $10 (b) $6
9. 52
10. $900
11. 7 h

12 (a) \$10.50 (b) 3 h
13. (a) 125° (b) 95° (c) 38°
14. 72°
15. 35°
16. \$8.50
17. \$148
18. 8

Exercise 53

1. 4 cm
2. (a) 6 cm (b) 7 cm (c) 4 cm
3. 3 cm
4. 2.5 m

Exercise 54

1. US 9 in. 3d *9 cm*
2. 13 cm

Exercise 55

1. 900 cm^3
2. 400 cm^3

Review 3

1. (a) 116 (b) 28
   (c) 71.2 (d) 0.056
2. 5.629
3. 0.01
4. 3.75
5. 64
6. 16.3
7. 2.44
8. $\frac{3}{5}$, $\frac{5}{7}$, $\frac{3}{4}$
9. 140 min
10. 1200 ml
11. 25%
12. 0.07
13. $\frac{9}{25}$
14. \$6
15. 75°
16. 32°
17. 40 cm^3
18. (a) US 30 $in.^2$ 3d *30 cm^2*
    (b) 3 : 7
19. (a) 150 ℓ (b) 250 ℓ
20. \$20
21. \$40